"YES!"

The dramatic life story of an Israeli woman who falls and raises again because of one word: "YES"!

Warning: This book can change your life

By Dominiquae Bierman

Copyright © 2008 by Dominiquae Bierman

"Yes!"
The dramatic life story of an Israeli woman who falls and raises again because of one word: "YES"!
by Dominiquae Bierman

Printed in the United States of America

ISBN 978-1-60647-987-2

All rights reserved solely by the author. The author guarantees all contents are original and do not infringe upon the legal rights of any other person or work. No part of this book may be reproduced in any form without the permission of the author. The views expressed in this book are not necessarily those of the publisher.

Unless otherwise indicated, Bible quotations are taken from The New American Standard version. Copyright © 2002 buy the Zondervan Corporation, used by permission. First Printing June 1996. www.biblegateway.com.

Contact details
www.dominiquaebierman.com
karenmap@netvision.net.il

Warning: This book can change your life

www.xulonpress.com

Dedicated

This book is dedicated to my beloved children Adi and Yuval who have been a blessing, a challenge and an inspiration in my life.

> *"All your sons will be taught of the LORD; and the well-being of your sons will be great."* Isaiah 54:13

Table Of Contents

Introduction xi

Chapter 1   Forbidden Waters 13

Chapter 2   Hidden Tears 17

Chapter 3   The Operation 21

Chapter 4   Land Of Our Ancestors 25

Chapter 5   The Big Escape 31

Chapter 6   Snapshots Of Adulthood 37

Chapter 7   Forever Mine 43

Chapter 8   Health, Health, Health! 49

Chapter 9   Yuval 53

Chapter 11 Adultery 65

Chapter 12 Demonic Freedom 71

Chapter 13 Light, Where Are You Lost?............................79

Chapter 14 The Light Of The World..................................85

Chapter 15 Yes!...89

Chapter 16 Born Again, Baby Steps 95

Chapter 17 Empowered By The Spirit.............................101

Chapter 18 Thy Kingdom Come, Thy Will Be Done 107

Chapter 19 Life Is Good 115

Chapter 20 The Still, Small Voice....................................121

Chapter 21 Dance For Joy...127

Chapter 22 A Mother's Heart..133

Chapter 23 The Lord Is My Shepherd 137

Chapter 24 Spiritual Warfare!...147

Chapter 25 Baruch 155

Chapter 26 A New Congregation In Israel!......................163

Chapter 27 The Letter Of The Law..................................169

Chapter 28 Meeting My Destiny.......................................181

Chapter 29 The Ugly Green Truck....................................191

Chapter 30 Dancing Down The Aisle 199

Epilogue	203
Contact Details	207
Other Books And Music Produced	209

Introduction

Dear Reader:

This book is a true story. Except for some occasions where I have changed names in order to protect the identity of some people, all other details are authentic. The reason for writing my life story to you is only one: LOVE. Not any kind of love, but a love that comes from heaven. That is, the love of God. I believe that many of you will identify with some of the things that happened to me, and if so, my prayer is that through the pages of this book you may find the One that rescued me, to whom I owe every breath and every second of my life.

    The way I wrote this book is a bit unconventional. It is designed to give you 'glimpses' and a open 'windows' into the story of my life. Or using another analogy, it is as if I have invited you into my home for a Shabbat evening, your free evening, and I host you to a 'finger food' buffet. Please relax, as we sit together in my comfortable living room and enjoy what could be a life changing story.

Chapter 1

Forbidden Waters

I was born to serve the God of my fathers. But at the time of my birth no one knew it. My mother had gone through a terrible pregnancy and very long hours of labor. Now, at last when my head was appearing the doctor turned pale.

"Quick! Bring me the scissors!" he shouted frantically at the nurse. My mother was barely conscious due to the pain, exhaustion and heavy medication.

I was blue and purple. I had swallowed a tremendous amount of meconium, (infant fecal matter in the birthing fluid). Even worse, the umbilical cord was wrapped so tightly around my neck that it was impossible to unwrap it.

With swift hands and an unction from God Almighty, the doctor made a precise cut of the cord around my neck, freeing me from deadly captivity. He proceeded to resuscitate me. I was more dead than alive and my chances of recovery were slight.

But God wanted me to live, so I lived! I was named Andrea Ronit (Ronit being my Hebrew name).

******

"Are you Jewish?" the teacher of catechism at the Catholic school asked.

"I don't know," I lied in a whisper, blushing from the tips of my ears. A holy hush fell on the classroom, as all the children knew I was Jewish and proud to be so.

"Well," the teacher said, with a dismissing wave of her hand, "You can stay as long as you sit quietly and behave yourself."

So I stayed.

I was six years old. We lived in Santiago, Chile where I heard only Spanish. My mother had enrolled me at the Breamer Catholic School as she wanted me to get the best English education available. My being Jewish hadn't seemed to pose a problem, for my parents' main purpose for me was not religious instruction but education. They knew that whenever it was time for classes on catechism, (Catholic religious studies), the teacher would ask all the Jewish girls to leave the room and play in the yard for that hour. This they did with explosive joy!

When the bells had rung for catechism time, Lillian Barros had shouted excitedly, "Come on, Andrea, we're free to play and jump rope. Come. Hurry! Why are you daydreaming?"

"No, Lillian," I had answered with determination. "I want to stay in my class and find out what this is all about."

Lillian sighed with frustration. "Do you always have to be so serious? Besides, what will your mom say? You know we are Jewish!" Shrugging her shoulders, she ran off. I had stayed in my chair, shy and a little frightened. The teacher of catechism was taking roll and did not recognize me. She raised an eyebrow and asked, "Are you a new student?" Not waiting for an answer she had asked the dreaded question, "Are you Jewish?"

I sat quietly, drinking in everything I could of this strange religion. It spoke of a Savior, of heaven, and of hell. It told about a man named Jesus Christ who was all man and all God. It was fascinating to dip into strictly forbidden waters!

As a Jew I was already in trouble. Even though my family was not religiously Jewish, we still bore deep wounds in our hearts from all the slaughters and pogroms done in one way or another in the name of Christ. The Nazi Holocaust was vivid in my parents' memory, in which six million Jews had been slaughtered in a supposedly Christian nation.

Little did I then know that the name "Christ" means "Messiah," and that he is mentioned countless times in my Jewish Bible!

It had been a good day at school. Once again I had spent another hour dipping into the forbidden waters of catechism. This God-man Jesus was beginning to be a personal friend to me. God the Father had become my Father too. I was excited. God was my friend, and He loved me! As I meditated on these strange things in my room at home, I was enveloped by a sweet, warmth and a tingling sensation of the reality of a Higher Nature.

"Andrea Ronit!" The distinctive voice of my mother brought me back to the mundane level.

"Yes, mom. I'm coming."

I ran from my bedroom to the living room where my mother, two smaller sisters and my brother, Ariel, were gathered. How I longed to communicate these things that were happening to me! But I concealed them in my heart, knowing they would not be understood.

"Andrea," said my mother in her no-nonsense voice, "Bring me all of your notebooks. I want to see how you are doing and what you are studying."

My heart froze! "Yes, mom," I said, trying to conceal the trembling in my voice.

My father was a university professor and spent long hours at work. When he came home that night my mom said, "Hiram, look!" She was indignant!

We were all in the room and with a distressed voice and shaking hands, she displayed before him what she had found — my catechism notebook! She flung the notebook open and there before us was a most vivid drawing of a bonfire. I had drawn it according to the teacher's requirement of a picture representing the fire of hell, showing how Jews and blacks and everyone who were not Catholics were going to be burnt in hell forever.

This clear hint of anti-Semitism, (hatred and discrimination of Jews,) caused my mom and dad to be in complete agreement.

"Tomorrow we will let the school know of our indignation," my mom said angrily.

"More than that," my dad said. "Register Andrea immediately at the Hebrew School, "Galvarino Gallardo". Let her start her Jewish education there at once!"

That night I sobbed under my covers. From tomorrow I would have to leave all my friends and that "special one," Jesus, who seemed to be the cause of all the problems. I was to be abruptly uprooted in order to be planted in completely new soil.

A new school, new friends, new subjects to learn. As I thought of all these things I grew quieter in my spirit. It was as if someone inside me had bathed me with peace and said, "It's okay, my baby. This is for my purposes. I will never leave you. Trust me!"

Chapter 2

Hidden Tears

"Get her!" Armando shouted.
"No. She's too quick. You get her, Alejandro! She's closer to you."

I was running for my life in the yard of the Hebrew school, "Galvarino Gallardo". Although the smallest in age and size in my class, I could outrun them all!

There were twelve students in the class. We studied, played and quarreled together for many hours a day. Ever since I had come to the school the year before, I had been almost the center of attention for both the students and teachers.

My poems depicting the magnificence of Chilean geography were hanging on the walls of the school. One of the girls, Miriam, became jealous of me because I also had a flair for drawing. She wanted to be "the queen of the class." Without my being aware of it, she thought that I held that "title." She would say little mean things from time to time that gradually made me aware of her jealousy.

I loved to sing, and in special functions would be asked to sing before the whole school. I delighted in physical education and gymnastics and was also one of the best students in the class, excelling in the Hebrew language and in study of the Bible, (the Tanach).

I felt very different from the other children, for I was serious and didn't take to the foolish games. Something inside me felt different although I didn't know what that something was.

******

We were four children in our home. My brother, Ariel, was the second child, a year and half younger than I. Vivi was three years younger than I, and Carolina six years younger.

Ariel was a very sensitive child. He was quiet most of the time, and had a pleasant nature. But from the time he was small, he had some emotional problems that developed later in life into a major problem.

My mother, though very warm and caring, had an abusive streak to her. She was a controversial woman.

On one hand she was caring, loving and compassionate. She eventually became a beautician, and ministered comfort and love to many who came for her services. She had a heart for people and loved to help. Many people would stream to her.

On the other hand she was cold, manipulative and controlling. Sometimes she was sweet and sometimes cruel, verbally and physically. She was deeply involved in the occult and witchcraft through meditation, Yoga and things of this nature.

Today I know that when people are involved in witchcraft and occult through different practices like yoga, meditation, Kabbala, spiritualism and even Freemasonry, etc. They caused them to be manipulative and controlling because of evil spirits that are involved in these practices. In one degree or another in our home we all had these tendencies, as our family had been some of these practices for generations.

My father was a brilliant man but he was not always at home. His career as a professor at the university caused him to work and study long hours. In many, many crucial times during our growing up, my dad was not there. He didn't know how to cope with many situations. The one who managed the household and our education was my mother. She carried most of the load, including the discipline.

We could sense some peace and love coming from him, but in many ways he was like a little boy. He tended to become angry very quickly, and then just as quickly appeased. He had the kind of personality that would flare up and then quiet down.

My mom and dad loved one another very much but had endless arguments about petty little things. I grew up with that constant bickering between them. It was normal for this strife and quarreling to be going on between them, and then again there would be love and embraces and hugs and kisses in front of us.

It was two extremes — tremendous passion and love for each other, yet tremendous strife and quarreling on the other hand. It was not violence with the use of hands, but verbal abuse, verbal put-downs, complaints, and manipulation to control situations. As I was growing up, I never felt that my dad was someone in whom I could find comfort or in whom I could confide.

On the other hand my father was a man of integrity. He was a man of his word, and whatever he said, he meant. He would research carefully before giving his opinion on things.

I learned from him that one's word is one's word, and we should not lie. My dad was not a man who lied. You could believe everything he said. Even though he was not an adequate father because he was absent in so many ways. At least as I was growing up as the firstborn in the family, he imparted to me a desire for truthfulness, trustworthiness and a willingness to research for established facts.

In spite of all their weaknesses my parents loved us and wanted the best for us and their lives were not always easy.

Chapter 3

The Operation

I heard the sound of commotion and a muffled cry of pain. "Hiram," said my mother, "We will have to search for better help than what we are getting here in Chile." My dad was in too much pain to answer. His kidneys had been failing for a while and the doctors in Chile had reached their capacity to help him. They had suggested for him to travel to the USA for a kidney operation. "But, the children..." said my dad in a strained voice. "My brother, Alfonso, will surely take care of them."

******

"Do you have to go, momma?" Ariel was asking. I was thinking to myself: "Will they ever come back?" Vivi was awfully quiet and had a frown on her little forehead. And Carolina, the baby, was not even there as she had been gravely ill with whooping cough and my maternal grandmother was taking care of her. I was six and a half when my parents drove away in an ambulance to board the plane that would take them to the USA for my father's kidney operation.

"How long will you be gone?" I had asked my mom. She looked intently into my eyes and said," I don't know."

Now we were in my uncle's home for an indefinite time. My aunt was trying to do her best but there was a chill in my heart. Many questions were going through my six-year-old mind. "Would dad live? Would they ever come back? Had my parents abandoned us?" A deep sense of abandonment started settling within my heart and as a little girl I decided that being self-reliant was very important for survival.

Six months later my parents came back knowing that father had been granted a miracle. He would live! He had not much left of his kidneys but he was alive and though still weak, he looked like a man who had been given a second chance. "He is a survivor. He refuses to leave me or the children alone", said my mother.

******

"Hi granny! Hi granddaddy! Here I am again!"

"Hello my darling," said grandma, "We were waiting for you for lunch".

Across the road from where we lived, in the apartment complex in Santiago, on a street called Carlos Antunez, were many buildings and apartments inhabited by Jewish people. Almost right opposite our home was an apartment complex where my maternal grandparents lived, my grandmother Susana and my grandfather Moises.

They had had a most successful business of making and selling woolen blankets. Their factory was burned down by someone trying to harm them but, undaunted, they collected the insurance and built another one. They were hard-working people with their own factory and business and always had enough for themselves and to help others financially.

My grandmother and grandfather did not get along very well. Their marriage had been arranged by a family member against the will of my grandmother, and she never got over that. But they seemed to manage to stay together.

For me it was very important that they were there, because, being the firstborn grandchild, I was the most pampered. They accepted me, loved me, and believed in me. It didn't matter what I did, they knew that I was intelligent, that I was going to make it, and that I was worthy of their attention.

There were many instances when I would spend weekends with them rather than my family. If I wanted any kind of comfort at all during my growing years, it would have to come from my grandmother. She became my special friend, and fed me special meals. One thing I really liked was avocado pears, and my grandmother fed me so many that I developed a reaction to them, and I cannot eat them anymore.

My grandmother was a very special lady. She always had a dedication to the poor people of this world. Many times she found children lost on the streets, or who had no food to eat. They would knock on her door and she would bring food out to them. Other times she would let them in to watch television in her house, or she would have them bathe and shower and then give them some good clothing.

That's the example I saw in my grandma's house.

I remember one conversation I had with her. She was feeding some children as I came into the house. She said, "Andrea, you can see that I'm doing what Jesus did."

"Oh," I said. "What did Jesus do?"

"Jesus fed the poor," she told me.

"Jesus was a very special man," she explained to me. "He was a man of compassion. He was a man of power, but he also was a man who loved the poor people, and he loved the ones who were downtrodden. I love Jesus because of that! He was a man of miracles, and he healed people."

On and on she told me about this Jesus, that I knew that he was all right. I knew that I had heard of him before, and had vague recollections about him from my Christian school and the religious classes I attended.

Though my grandmother was a Jew she accepted Christianity as a religion and she accepted Jesus as a man that came from God to help and to give. She was an example of someone who is open-minded.

Chapter 4

Land Of Our Ancestors

"Havenu shalom aleichem, havenu shalom aleichem..." We children were all singing together on board the ship as we approached the coast of Israel. The ship had already passed through the Mediterranean Sea and was nearing our beloved Promised Land, Israel.

Although I was only 11 years old I had gathered the children together. We were sitting at the front of the ship. This was an event of great importance to us all, and we sang heartily in celebration of our memorable arrival in Haifa, Israel.

I was proud to be a Jew! I was proud that my father had finally fulfilled his promise that we would one day emigrate to Israel as citizens. Israel had proclaimed "the Law of Return" that automatically accepts every Jew into the land with full citizenship. My father was the leader of part of this group, leading them into their biblical inheritance. What a joy!

During the month-long boat travel to our first stop in Italy, my relationship with my family was strained. There we boarded another ship which took us directly to Israel.

My younger brother Ariel had been seriously ill throughout the trip with a raging fever, and we were aware of the horrible possibility that he might not be alive by the end of the trip. He spent the whole month in the ship hospital, but I had become so disassociated from the family that I didn't visit him except once. This was strange, as I loved my brother dearly. My brother was totally helpless, and, we who were close to him couldn't help him much either. Yet my mother tended and cared for him day and night.

My family was really disappointed with me. It was as if for some unknown reason I didn't really belong, and I felt more and more distant, with little communication or understanding between us.

Twenty-five years later I visited Chile with my husband, Baruch. As I was lying on the beach of Reniaca on the coast of the Pacific, where we used to spend the most beautiful summers with the paternal side of my family, including cousins, aunts and uncles, I understood why I became so alienated from the family.

It was a defense mechanism against the pain of separation, as we had just "cut off" our ties with our family in Chile, especially my maternal grandparents. In order to cope with it, I grew estranged from my parents who were the cause of the separation as they took us to Israel. Though I was in total agreement with their decision, my heart had suffered and had found a way to deny the pain. A denial that went on for 25 years!... until that day on the beach.

Yet at the time of arrival at Haifa port we were all utterly excited. Finally, we had arrived at the land of our ancestors!

******

Settling in a new country was very stressful for us. For the first five months we were assigned to stay at the Jewish absorption center in Netanya, which is between Haifa and Tel Aviv. Its purpose was to absorb the new immigrants, help them find jobs and to learn the Hebrew language in a day school called the *ulpan*.

"Yes!"

Our family was quite different from many of the others at the center. Most of the families were complaining about the hardships, as they had become accustomed to a comfortable life in Chile. But my parents had a good pioneer spirit, so our family adjusted well to the new culture, and loved it.

"I won't touch her!"

"I won't touch her either!"

"Get away from her!"

I was as rejected and despised as a leper! Some of the boys at the absorption center had begun forming a circle in order to learn some steps of Israeli folk dancing, but they wouldn't let me into the circle.

The reason for their rejection was this stupid game in which everyone had to reveal his or her romantic inclinations. In that game all the boys had discovered that they were in love with me, but since I wasn't "in love" with any of them, they began a cruel warfare of rejection against me.

Even though I had gone through much rejection at the Hebrew school in Chile for being different and talented, this new bout of rejection caught me by surprise. Although I was only 11 years old, my budding femininity seemed to attract the boys like flies. By not responding to their feelings I was in trouble.

The experience of being rejected for being different or being more gifted in certain areas, followed me constantly as a painful shadow all through my childhood and teenage years.

I am thankful that at school I was loved and cherished, where again I was the smallest in age and in size. I was better accepted by the Israelis of Mizrachi origin than by the Ashkenazi. These Mizrachi Jews were warm and hospitable from the outset. Mizrachi Jews in Israel were of eastern or oriental origin — from Arabic countries like Morocco, Iran, Iraq, etc. The Ashkenazi Jews were mostly of European origin.

******

By the age of twelve, I realized that I could not count on my father as a good provider. Financially speaking, there would be provision for food and there would be basic clothing, but if I needed anything more than that — any type of need, such as a little more clothing, or something different or special, he wasn't the person I could go to. That made a big impression on me. I grew further away from my family, and this situation carried on into my teenage years. There would be no real communication or understanding between us.

At age twelve I started working, baby-sitting, and doing every kind of seasonal work possible to have my own money. Actually, I became the one in the family who had pocket money when others didn't. I became a provider, and could provide in many ways. That pattern has accompanied me through life.

******

His big imposing figure appeared at the entrance to the classroom. A solemn hush fell over us as we all quickly gave our full attention to Dr. Shefy. He was the high-school principal in Miterani High School in Holon, a town south of Tel Aviv.

"Christianity," he said, with no introduction, "is an exciting religion. It is a collection of many sects and denominations that fight yet complement one another. The roots of Christianity are Jewish roots. This religion came out of Judaism nearly 2000 years ago. If it hadn't been for Judaism, Christianity would be non-existent today."

"A Jewish man by the name of Saul of Tarsus who eventually changed his name to Paul the Apostle, applied himself to the spread of Christianity throughout most of the civilized world, including Greece, Macedonia and eventually Rome. Therefore the Christians owe their roots to the Jews."

******

The noise of moving chairs was quite deafening as we all endeavored to form a circle with them. There was excitement in the air! Yosi was coming to address us concerning his role in the 1973 Yom Kippur War.

He was a courageous soldier who had received medals because of his courage, as he was terribly wounded while fighting on the Syrian border.

This was the end of 1976, and my last year in high school. I was sixteen and a half, the youngest of all my graduating class.

Yosi came in, dressed in his military attire and sat down among us. I looked at him with admiration. My heart throbbed because of the love I had for my country, and for the men who defended it. Soon I would be a soldier too. I would do my patriotic share in its defense.

"You are all very important to Israel," he said. "You are the new generation we can count on to defend and build this country."

We all sat straight on our chairs, listening soberly and intently.

"There are many things to do. We need to settle the West Bank of the Jordan River with Jewish settlers, so that the world understands finally that God, in the Bible, gave us all of the Promised Land. And that includes what anti-Israeli sources call 'the occupied territories.' These are not 'the occupied territories,' children. These are the liberated territories. In the 1973 war, after we were stealthily attacked on our holiest day of the year, the Day of Atonement, Yom Kippur, we conquered these territories and brought them

"Yes!"

back to Israel. These territories are part of our biblical inheritance. There is much opposition politically, but I am calling the youths of Israel to rise up and demonstrate that they have a voice! This country has strong, vibrant, patriotic future soldiers — that will not give up!"

I screamed "YES!" My heart was leaping out of my chest. I will go as part of the vision. My country, Israel, will never be given back — never!! After 2000 years of exile and persecutions suffered by us Jews, it would be an act of suicide to give our inheritance back.

Many other youngsters were stirred up with me. We were zealous and full of fire. We would defend our country whatever it would take!

Yosi explained what had happened to him during the war. He showed us many scars and wounds. His face was disfigured. Bullets had pierced him through like a colander. Yet he was still alive and was regarded as a miracle.

I looked at the disfigured young man. I couldn't see anything but a radiant beauty of one who had given up his life for my beloved country.

I knew then that whatever it takes, I was willing to give my life for my country too!

Chapter 5

The Big Escape

It was one of those crisp Israeli mornings in Batyam, the southern suburb of Tel Aviv. Dad and mom summoned us all into the family room of the small apartment where the six of us lived.

"We're going to Mexico in August, at the latest," dad said, "to spend a year or two in that country. I have been invited to establish a new department of Cynematics* in the biggest university of Mexico City, Universidad Nacional Autonoma de Mexico [U.N.A.M.]."

"The Israeli government has made a decision," my mother added, "to have your father be part of an exchange program between Israel and Mexico. It is a great honor for your father to be sent to represent Israel in the area of scientific exchange."

I was delighted to hear this, for I truly love traveling. I was now 17 years old and had finished high school. Army enrollment is mandatory for young men and women at 18, but I was too young.

*Cynematics concerns the movement of robotic arms for industry.

I had already received special permission from the Israeli army to delay enrollment for another three years.

This would provide time for me to get my bachelor's degree in English and French literature. Then the army would take me through an officer's course and I would be able to serve in a senior position, due to my academic education. But at this point, traveling to Mexico sounded like a once-in-a-lifetime opportunity to see more of the world. Since I spoke Spanish fluently due to my Chilean origin, I could continue my studies in Mexico, if I joined my family in this exchange program.

My mother used to be very resourceful. Between us we succeeded in pulling all the needed strings to get a miraculous permission from the Israeli army for me to leave the country temporarily. Was I ever happy when all that bureaucracy was behind me!

One of my best friends at the Tel Aviv University was Deena, who had been born in Mexico. She came from an affluent Jewish family in Mexico City, which moved in Jewish social circles there. She was to be back in Mexico that summer. She offered to introduce me to her friends and to acquaint me with the best that Mexico City could offer.

It was ten o'clock at night when the plane landed in Mexico City. We were all dizzy and extremely tired, due not only to jet lag but also to the high altitude of the city. We checked into the Hotel El Presidente, where all six of us collapsed onto our respective beds, completely exhausted.

What is that? Half awake, I listened. Knock, knock, knock. "Ronit, open. It's Deena! I'm taking you to breakfast." I got dressed quickly, scribbled a hurried note to my sleeping family and off Deena and I went through the very busy streets of Mexico City.

The first thing I noticed was the tremendous smog. It covered the city like a thick, threatening cloud. I could hardly breathe, but the thrill of being in a new country took over, and I felt happy and expectant.

"Yes!"

Once we were sitting in the coffee shop we started chatting as only two schoolmates would do. "I'll introduce you to all my friends," said Deena. "They are already waiting for you. And I have a surprise for you! My best friend Sandy is getting married, and I've already arranged a date for you. Oscar is handsome, and very rich. He'll pick you up in his black sports car. It's a Mercedes. I want you to dress as elegantly as you can!"

Life is not bad after all, I thought to myself. Out loud I said, "Deena, tell me a little about the U.N.A.M. You know I'll be studying there in a few days."

Deena, being very eloquent and able to speak rapidly, gave me a quick verbal picture of the nature of the university. "It's the most exciting campus," she said. "Things are happening all the time. Students spend more time in parades, protest marches and political crusades than in studying. Yesterday for example, they were marching with flaming torches."

"For what purpose?" I asked.

"Who knows?" she said.

Being a patriotic Israeli I was used to fighting for clear causes. I had lived through one major war in 1973 on the Day of Atonement, which is the holiest day of the year for the Jewish people. I was fourteen at that time. We were taught to be aware of the danger of being surrounded by hostile Arab nations. As an Israeli youth, I had grown up with a strong sense of purpose in my life: to protect my country, contributing to its building and the formation of a free Jewish society. For young students to be spending their time in political rallies for no clear reason seemed foolish to me.

"Andrea, are you ready?" called my sister. It was about time to go to the Folklorical Penia which features Mexican music and drama. One of the main musicians in the band was also the assistant to the professor in the physics department at the U.N.A.M. He had invited our father and all of us as special guests.

I was down from my "roof-top" bedroom in a jiffy. "All ready to go," I said.

We packed into the car and were off through the busy streets of Mexico City. As we came into the small room of the theater where the performance was to be held, we walked into a cloud of cigarette smoke! The lights were dim, and the atmosphere very charged. The sweet voice of a singer was singing "Alfonsina y el mar," a very romantic and typical Mexican song.

After the performance, I was personally introduced to one of the lead singers. His name was Juan Pablo, the famous assistant to the professor at the physics department. He was bright, had sung magnificently, and was very romantic. But he was not particularly handsome; being overweight from the large quantities of liquor he often drank to overcome depression.

But at that time I knew nothing of his drinking or his depression. We fell head over heels in love.

"Andrea, who are you making these sandwiches for?" inquired my suspecting mom. I was in the kitchen, hurriedly preparing some sandwiches for Juan Pablo and myself. We had planned to spend some time together in between school hours.

"Andrea, this relationship is getting too serious," my mother added. "You know he is not Jewish, but Catholic. You're supposed to go back to Israel to serve in the army. Remember? This is getting to be dangerous...." She was very concerned, and rightly so.

The pressure at home against this relationship became extremely bad. Every one in the family agreed that things were moving too fast between Juan and I.

But in the heat of youth and foolish romance, Juan Pablo and I prepared a "big escape." We would just elope and get married, against all opposition!

"Yes!"

******

Quickly, I thought, I'll just pack one night gown, two skirts, my two best sweaters, my sandals, and some underwear. Oh yes, and my spare toothbrush. Hmmm.... I think it wouldn't be too obvious if I had taken just a few books with me.

I was really nervous about my "roof top" room with my sister Vivi, for she could come in at any minute and spoil all our plans for eloping.

Just then she burst into the room. "What are you doing, Andrea?"

"Shhhhhh! Don't make so much noise, Vivi! I'm leaving! Juan Pablo and I are getting married. And don't you dare say a word to anyone or I will kill you!"

My sister, though three years younger, didn't have a real appreciation for romance, nor did she believe my threats. Before the hour was over, my parents were fully informed. I couldn't make a move that night.

"Are you pregnant?" my conservative father asked. We were sitting in a beautiful shaded spot of nature, when my parents decided to have a talk with me.

"No," I said, "that's not the reason for this marriage." I was deeply touched by my father's openness and desire for real communication between us. Often during my teen years I just withdrew and lived my life as if I weren't a part of the family. I had learned to be very guarded in my emotions and in my heart.

My mother was crying. "If you marry him, you'll never be able to raise your children in Israel!"

That touched a sore spot in my heart, so we negotiated a "peace treaty." I agreed to postpone the wedding decision until we had come back from a month long trip to Chile that we had planned. We wanted to visit the family we had left behind when we emigrated to Israel seven years earlier. I loved my grandmother and grandfather dearly, and was eager to see them again.

While in Chile I did a lot of thinking and made a few decisions. (1) My relationship with Juan Pablo was not true love, but a foolish infatuation. (2) The wedding needed to be cancelled in the most careful way possible, as Mexican men have a reputation for violence, especially concerning romantic affairs. I was afraid he might want to kill me. (3) I decided that as soon as we arrived back in Mexico City, I should arrange to leave for Israel immediately, and enroll in the army in order to fulfill my duty to my country.

"We'll be landing in Mexico City in a few minutes. All passengers are required to stop smoking and fasten their seat belts."

My heart was still rehearsing the explanation I had to give Juan Pablo on calling off of our wedding. Still ringing in my ears were his earnest words, telling me he was willing to leave his country in order to go and live with me in Israel.

The plane landed. I followed through on my decisions.

Chapter 6

Snapshots Of Adulthood

"Smol Yemin, Smol Yemin....March, One, Two, stop!" I was giving marching orders to my girls, in Hebrew, of course. There was dust everywhere and it was getting to be hot, but I had a purpose. I had the responsibility of training a "fresh batch" of civilian women and, along with others, turn them into disciplined soldiers in a month's time. Every month there were 50 new faces, 50 new lives to touch.

"Dismissed for lunch! Go!"

I hadn't chosen to do this. After I came back from Mexico I had immediately enrolled in the army. I had no problem adjusting to the army discipline. The chief commander of the base had interviewed me about becoming a trainer at the base. I wasn't very happy about it, as it is one of the toughest jobs assigned to a female soldier. It required a lot, physically and emotionally.

The commander said to me, "We only choose the 'cream of the crop'."

I was honored, though still not sure that I would be tough enough for the job. Soon enough I found myself taking the trying three months' training course.

******

"She's coming! She's coming!" yelled "my" girls in warning each other. I had entered the building for the weekly inspection of their living quarters. I was now in my second year of service in the armed forces and had been given a very rewarding job in the air force. I had been placed in charge of the entire female population of the base. I was the second in command, being a sergeant under the resident women's officer. She had given me complete freedom in my job.

I knocked on the door. "Anybody home?" I called in a loud voice.

Slowly a tired looking woman in her mid-forties opened the door. "Shalom," I said, extending my hand to her. "I am your daughter, Shoshana's, army commander."

"Come in, come in," she said.

We sat in the tiny living room on a chair that had seen better days. The whole atmosphere of the house seemed terribly oppressive. The mother showed me a bottle with many different pills. "This is for depression," she said. "This is to calm anger, this is for heart palpitations, and this is for diabetes. I suffer a lot," she added. "Now my daughter has tried to commit suicide again. We don't know what to do with her!"

Shoshana had been in rebellion and had been absent from the base for a few days. It was my duty, among other things, to make house calls and evaluate hard cases before the military police came to arrest them and take them to military jail to discipline them. I would be the one visiting them in jail later, and would be involved in the process of helping them straighten up their life. This would be through conversations, personal counseling, personal example, and as a last resort, through punishment.

This was an invaluable time of training for me in learning to understand people and their intricate problems, but there were never enough tools.

"Yes!"

******

"Hold tight, now steady! One, two, three... shoot!" Off went a swift number of bullets out of the "Uzy" submachine gun.

"Not bad!" I yelled to the man who was doing the shooting. "You almost got the heart of the target!"

My job now was to retrain all the people in this Air Force base in using their personal weapons. It was a refresher course even for all the high ranking officers. I was honored to be the one asked to do it. It would cause the whole base to shape up, and it was quite a task. I carried it out with joy and pride.

But while all these things were happening, something else was beginning. Someone had decided to target me.

The telephone in my office kept ringing persistently. This was strange, since most of the offices in the base were closed, as it was now after hours. Who would know that I was still there?

"Hello, who is it?"

"It's me," answered a subdued male voice from the other end of the line. "My name is Yoram. I met you in the shuttle bus, and I know that you are working after hours. As a matter of fact, I know a lot about you."

It sounded "creepy," yet it aroused my curiosity. We made a date and became just friends, as I did not allow any relationship to distract me from my responsibilities in the armed forces. I was highly respected, and wanted no stains on my reputation.

It was dark in his office, and he had noticed the light in mine. "Here she is again," he had thought, "I can see her office from here. I'm going to get her, whatever it takes! I will get her! She will be mine!" And with such manipulative determination he proceeded to conjure a most ingenious plan.

In a few months we were in front of a solemn rabbi in the beautiful Ben Yehuda synagogue in Tel Aviv, saying, "I do" in the presence of friends and family.

My mother looked miserable, as she had the feeling that this marriage would end in disaster. A few days earlier, foreseeing some problems, she had said, "If you want to, and you are in doubt, we could cancel the wedding."

"Oh mom," I replied. "All the invitations have been sent. It's too late!"

A year and six months later we were divorced.

******

On the way to adulthood I had lost some moral standards. At the age of 17, before we had left for Mexico City, I lost my virginity due to my intense desire to become like everybody else. The experience was exceedingly traumatic for me, for it crushed my wall of dignity as a woman and left deep scars. This was the door that had led me to a loss of standards. Now, after my divorce, I found myself "rooming-in" with a very handsome and sensitive young man whom I will call Danny.

He was intelligent, sweet, full of potential yet lacking in achievements, for there was a dark shadow in his recent past that I did not know about. He had experienced a horrible mental illness called manic-depression.

Yet when I met him he was doing well. He had a heart of gold, loved to help everybody, and was finishing his requirements for becoming a government-licensed, Israeli tour guide. We decided to get married.

"Do you know who you are marrying?" Danny's father resounded inquisitively. I was sitting beside Danny, and as usual we were having a very friendly conversation. I giggled.

"Of course I do!" I responded, with tremendous self-assurance. "We've been together now for a year and a half!"

The question had seemed peculiar, coming from the lips of this man whom I was learning to respect and admire. The question had a hidden meaning. Fragments of past conversations began echoing in my mind, phrases such as: "Danny was depressed for eight months." "The doctors called it manic-depression." "Lithium was suggested but he refused to take it." "Then he became manic, boastful, squandering thousands of dollars on crazy business ventures." "It could happen anytime, or it might not happen again." "All this started after the 1973 war and the loss of his best friend."

Chapter 7

Forever Mine

"All units are called to present themselves to their nearest army base. Repeat: all units...."

The radio announcer spoke with urgency in his voice. War again! The Lebanese border had been a thorn-in-the-flesh for years. Terrorists infiltrated across the border and slaughtered innocent civilians. This terror was happening continually for the people living in the settlements along the Galilee-Lebanese border. Machine-gun shells and missiles were launched across the border every other day. What had begun as a commando-unit assignment that would put a stop to this cruel cycle of events had turned into a major war. "The war for the peace of Galilee" had started.

These were the first days of June, 1982, and we had set the date for a delightful wedding ceremony and reception on the 7th of June.

The telephone rang. "Yes, I understand," Danny spoke into the receiver in a hurried tone. I will be there as soon as possible."

I looked at him. "You have to report immediately for service, don't you?" He nodded very seriously. "I'll come with you," I said, perking up, "and talk to your army commander to allow you time off to get married!"

In no time we were in the car, heading for the Lower Galilee area where he had to report for duty. I was dressed extravagantly, since we had just come home from a party when the phone call had come. It was one o'clock in the morning.

"Thank you! Thank you!" I grabbed this muscular, well-composed man, hugged him and kissed him on the cheek.

"Did you see that?" whispered many of the soldiers who were sitting around waiting for instructions. "The commander is blushing all over!"

I was oblivious to the stares. I was just genuinely grateful that in spite of the urgency of the situation, Danny and I were allowed time off to get married and to spend three days together after the wedding before he had to report for duty. This was nothing short of a miracle!

Ever since then there has been a story circulating within that army unit about "the time when the commander lost his poise."

Lights all over the trees! What a night! June is a good month for garden weddings in the northern suburbs of Tel Aviv. This was the beautiful garden of my precious new parents-in-law, whom I loved and appreciated. They lived in one of the most expensive neighborhoods of the whole of Israel. Diplomats made their homes here. It was and is, a coveted place to live in.

I was happy. This time my mom was happy too. At last this was the right man, and the right family, and certainly the right place for a wedding.

Both Danny and I were dressed in off-white, and my future mother-in-law, who was sparing in her compliments, said that we looked like movie stars! My hair was flowing loosely over my shoulders, ribboned with small jasmine flowers. We looked fresh, rich, vibrant and young.

"Yes!"

A holy hush filled the garden as the famous television figure, Rabbi Avidor Hacohen, motioned with his hands for quietness, to begin this sacred ceremony.

This time it's forever, my heart said.

"Will you take...for better or for worse...." the rabbi intoned.

"I do!" Danny replied.

"I do!" said I, with quiet confidence.

******

"Quick! Hook her up to the monitor! She's not dilating enough! Bring Dr. Chen (not the real name). Dr. Chen is in charge today."

So many tubes, so many hands, so much noise, and the only thing I wanted to do was to give birth in peace! I had even brought my knitting with me to the hospital after the contractions had started, and I had painted my nails, (yes, even my toenails), in order to be pretty for this joyous event — the birth of my first child! Among all the birthing mamas in the waiting room, I had been the only one with a smile. Danny and I had prepared ourselves for natural childbirth. We were confident.

"A cesarean? No!" I said. "I will give birth naturally!"

"Do you want to kill your baby?" the doctor asked, threateningly. All the medical students gathered around me were nodding their heads in approval of the doctor's words. "You have a clear case of cpd," the doctor said, "which means that your pelvis is too narrow for you to give birth naturally."

The thought flashed across my mind, "Didn't God create women to give birth?" But no one listened to any of my objections.

"You're a good soldier!" the anesthesiologist encouraged. "Now, this epidural will just numb your lower parts, but you will be conscious —."

An hour later I was brought a bundle. "What's her name?" they asked me.

I couldn't see her and they didn't allow me to touch her. "Quick," I said to myself, "I need a name!" My heart said, "I wish I could touch her!" "The name is Adi," I told them after a moment. And away they took her as if she didn't belong to me at all.

"Andrea," said my concerned mom as she sat beside my bed, "don't worry. You'll be out of the hospital in a week and I'll help you take care of Adi."

My mom was trying to comfort me, as I looked so sad. I had learned as a child that I had to be strong to withstand the hard blows of life. My past experiences as a sick child with my mother had taught me that weakness was not tolerated.

I did not know then that as a little girl my mother had felt rejected by her mother, the same grandmother who was so good to me as a little girl. My mother carried wounds of rejection that only God could some day heal.

Now, here in my great disappointment, my mother was ministering to me in a very special way!

"Mom," I said, "I have a daughter whom I haven't touched, or seen, or nursed — and I wish I could!" I was at the point of tears. I was connected to a few machines, one of them an IV, and looked rather pitiful. My breasts were exploding with milk and I needed to feed my baby.

My courageous and resourceful mom borrowed a white nurse's gown, and in no time, as if by a miracle, she was wheeling a hospital baby carriage down the hall to my room with a tiny sleeping bundle inside. She lifted the baby up and presented Adi to me.

My daughter! How beautiful, she is full of soft dark hair and white complexion with healthy, rosy cheeks. I checked

"Yes!"

---

her carefully all over, fingers and toes. Delicate features, a true princess, an Eve. The nurses said later on that she was one of the most beautiful babies ever born in that hospital.

Adi means Jewel. It also means, "Forever mine!"

Chapter 8

Health, Health, Health!

"Shalom!" I said to the saleslady. "Do you have soy milk and could you give me some advice about milk allergies?" I had gone into the local health-food store in the little town of Herzelia where Danny, Adi and I lived.

The woman looked as puzzled as if I had asked her how to go to China from Israel. She obviously didn't know much about nutrition. I turned to Danny and whispered in his ear, "I could be a health-food store owner easily. I'm better informed than this lady!" He quietly agreed with me.

In less than two months I was opening my first health-food store. My beloved father-in-law invested a sum of money to help me start it. He was confident that I could run it successfully.

Danny's profession was tourism, but he was a freelance tour guide and didn't have much work during certain times of the year. So he helped look after Adi, and he would bring her to me for breast-feeding. My store was only five minutes away from home.

It became a real success. I became knowledgeable about nutrition, health and the human body in general. I also enrolled in "The School of Natural Health" in Tel Aviv, and took studies all the way up to a Ph.D. in health and nutrition. Life was good to me!

"Ronit," said Danny one day. "Why don't you work as a tour guide also? You are licensed and know all these languages. You can do it. and it's excellent money!"

Adi had weaned herself from the breast as she turned a year old. My store was doing great, as I had a faithful and talented store manager to help me. My mother-in-law was a wonderful help with Adi and was delighted to look after her.

I agreed with Danny, and before I knew it I found myself housekeeping, mothering, tour guiding, studying (nutrition), managing a store and giving nutritional counseling. I was 24 years old, in vibrant health, full of faith and thought that life could never be better.

There were a few problems between Danny and me, but I chose to ignore them, since I was so busy and self-fulfilled.

It was hot, hot, and hotter — a typical Israeli summer. I was in Jerusalem with 50 tourists, carrying a flag, a pointer and wearing a big hat.

I stopped, motioning everyone to halt right there. "Look in front of you," I said, at the top of my lungs. "These men dressed in black are orthodox, religious Jews. Even though it is hot, they always wear their heavy black coat. They are praying to the God of Israel. This is the Most Holy site for us Jews. Over there is where the temple used to be. This is the famous Wailing Wall. People come from all over the world to put their prayer requests in the cracks between the stones of the wall. You can expect miracles! God answers prayers here!"

Everyone was excited. They had been waiting for this moment since the beginning of the tour. The view was magnificent. The Mount of Olives was on the right, the Temple Mount to the left, the golden Dome of the Rock on top, and down below was the pearl of Judaism: the Wailing Wall, built of big white limestones, the Jerusalem stone.

"Before I let you write your prayer requests," I told them, "I want you to listen to me." A holy hush fell over the group, and I explained, "Jesus Christ did his Bar Mitzva right here where the Temple used to be. You'd better know from now on that he was born Jewish!"

I just had to say it!

"Did you hear what she said?" whispered one lady to another.

"I've always thought of Jesus as Catholic," the other one replied. Then she added, "Now that I think about it, it's been a long time since I've read my Bible."

"Did you notice how much she knows about our Jesus? But of course if he was born Jewish he might mean something to her as well. Hmmmm, interesting!"

******

"Do you see my arm?" This good-looking lady from South Africa showed me an ugly scar. "I suffered from cancer two years ago and the Lord healed me miraculously."

"The Lord?" I asked. "Do you mean God?"

She laughed, and said hurriedly, "Yes, God."

We were sitting on our spacious terrace in a large apartment that Danny and I were renting. These ladies were his guests. He had been their tour guide for 10 days. They had been eager to meet me.

Before they came Danny had told me, "You're going to love them. They are very spiritual, and when they worship Jesus they fall into a trance and pray in a language called 'tongues.' They seem to be in love with Jesus, and seem to love everyone else too. It is strange, I tell you!"

And then the God of Israel spoke to these women, his daughters, as they arrived safely back in South Africa after their outstanding tour in the Holy Land. "Pray for your Jewish, Israeli sister," God told them. "I am calling her to myself."

Chapter 9

Yuval

"How wonderful, Mrs. F." said the most popular and expensive obstetrician of the Sharon area. Or at least I thought he was. "I'm going to schedule you for your next cesarean operation."

I was not even a month pregnant. "You're what?" I asked, perplexed.

"Well, you know, 'once a cesarean always a cesarean' is the rule. You have a cpd problem you know. You pelvis is too narrow for any kind of birthing."

"Dear doctor," I told him, "my body was created perfectly for giving birth, and I will give birth at home, with or without you!"

"It will be without me then," he said.

I thanked him politely and left the office, indignant.

Pant — pant — breathe, breathe. — Relax. Contraction — breathe — pain —. Danny had been faithfully tending to me, running hot and cold water on my spine to ease the pain. I refused to take the conventional poisonous medication. Just as I had planned, I was giving birth at home.

My midwife was of Jewish-American origin, and a brave lady. She was once again putting her career in jeopardy by assisting not only in a home birth, but a home birth for someone who had had a previous cesarean.

No machines. No medications, no unnecessary hands checking and rechecking my cervical dilation. With loving hands she massaged my aching lower back. Though dilation was as slow as in my first labor, she allowed the natural process to continue. I had faith that God had created my body perfectly for giving birth.

Later during the labor we would have the assistance of a very cooperative and sympathetic obstetrician who was willing to risk his professional standing in order to help in this home birth.

I had prepared myself physically with excellent nutrition and had been swimming nearly every morning an average of 40 laps, in an Olympic-size swimming pool.

During the last few weeks of pregnancy I had tried to put my business in order. I had just opened my second health-food store and was trying to find a competent manager. This was no small task, because this store was bigger and had three levels. The upper floor was established as my private nutritional counseling office. I was gaining fame as a much sought-after nutritionist. I wrote a monthly column in the local women's magazine, and this generated good publicity. I had been in my office until the contractions began.

"Puush! Here is the head, now slowly, —"

I was half seated with many cushions behind my back and I could see everything. — Here he was! My first boy! Yuval!

He was bigger than Adi, yet he came out naturally with no problems. His head had shaped itself in the form of my pelvis and he came out smoothly.

He did not cry. With his eyes wide open he looked at me peacefully as if to say, "God sent me to tell you that you were right!" He fell asleep on my breast. He was a handsome, sturdy little boy, yet he nursed gently.

"Yes!"

My wonderful baby son and I were in total agreement. God had created my body perfectly for birthing. What a joy!

"Baruch ata Adonai Elohenu Melech Haolam, Bore Shamaym Ve arets uvoreh headam bitsalmo,..." The Mohel was chanting the blessings and preparing his tools for the ancient ceremony of circumcision, the cutting of the foreskin, or the Brit Mila, which means, "The Covenant of Circumcision". The same covenant that God made with Abraham thousands of years ago.

My son Yuval was eight days old, according to the requirement of the law of circumcision that God spoke of in the Bible. He was oblivious of everyone, lying down peacefully on the table, set for this occasion; for this most solemn ceremony.

People had gathered from both sides of the family along with some of our faithful friends and they were all high in anticipation.

Oh my God! I thought to myself. They are going to cut my son! Is all this really necessary?

Up in the heavens, the Messiah of Israel rose from his Holy Throne. Another Jewish boy was entering into Covenant with him. God was pleased!

"Amen!" It was done. They handed me my shocked and crying bundle, and everyone was rejoicing. The foreskin had been cut off.

Doctors say that it's been discovered that it is healthier this way and that it even protects against cancer in the male organ. It's been proven. But as a mother I just wanted to comfort my son! I did not know that this was a foreshadowing of the New Covenant that God had made with my son 2000 years ago in Jerusalem.

Yuval was named after the first musician in the Bible (Genesis 4:21). His name also means a stream, or tributary that flows out of the main river.

"And he showed me a pure river of water of life, clear as crystal, proceeding out of the throne of God and of the Lamb." (Revelation 22:1)

Chapter 10

The Downfall

I screamed at Danny, "If there is no change in you by your birthday next year, something terrible will happen!" I was beside myself!

Danny had fallen into a devastating state of depression. This was his birthday. I had given him a surprise party and had invited all his favorite friends, to prove to him that he was loved by many. I had hired a high-class entertainer and had cooked a luscious health food buffet for nearly 20 people. Yuval was four months old and breast-feeding steadily. I was exhausted!

Danny had spent the entire evening curled under the big dining room table behaving like an animal in distress. He had refused to take any medication for his condition. He just refused help.

We had spent many sleepless nights together having the most peculiar conversations. "Everything will be destroyed, you know," he would repeat several times. "We're in a big overdraft at the bank. Your stores will surely collapse!"

Or he would say, "There's just no hope! Everything is dark," and on and on and on for endless hours in the night, night after night.

"Mrs. F.," the doctor said, "I advise you to confine your husband to a mental institution. At least he will have supervision there."

My heart froze, for the words "mental institution" sounded like a death sentence to me! Hadn't my dear younger brother, Ariel, spent the past seven years in mental institutions? He had never looked any better to me in all that time. He was still confined. I felt that if I agreed to this for Danny, he too would never come out again. He would stay there forever, taking the most obnoxious drugs.

"No," I said, "I'll make sure that he takes his medication at home."

The doctor, a Jewish psychologist of Argentinean Jewish origin looked at me with concerned eyes and handed me the prescription.

In spite of all the problems I loved Danny more than my own life, and I wanted him well.

There were many stars that night. There was a clear August sky. It was an Israeli summer in its utmost beauty. Cleona, my South African helper who was a real Godsend to me, had helped me put the two children to bed.

Danny was confined to our bedroom, as usual in those days. He was not working nor reading, but his mind going in circles. Adi didn't understand why her daddy was so different from the way he had been before. Yuval didn't even know his daddy, as there had been so little contact between the two of them. Danny used to be a very warm father, but this depressive state had nullified all of his good intentions.

I was sitting on our terrace smoking my daily cigarette. Since I knew smoking was a killer, I'd just indulge in one or two at the end of the day. It was a kind of ritual that represented the exhausted end of yet another hopeless day.

I put my feet up on the chair in front of me. "God," I said, looking at the stars, "if you are there some place, heal my husband." I felt a clear sense that I had been heard.

"Yes!"

******

"So you found a black chicken that lays eggs," the rabbi said. "Take one egg and break it at the entrance to your apartment. This is for his sexual problems. Then take some soil, and...." On and on he went! This was a peculiar man, this was a cabalistic rabbi! He knew through an occult practice called numerology that Danny and I had been sexually incompatible from the start, for Danny had almost no sexual drive whatsoever. As a wife I had been rejected and denied sex for the last six years. It was by a sheer miracle that we managed to have two gorgeous children.

I had compensated for the lack of sex with a lot of hard work, business and studies. When tourism was low, Danny could not be the provider of the family, so I had become the one providing and pulling the financial load. It was good that I had learned as a girl to become self-reliant and not to depend on others. I knew even then that if I worked hard enough I would make it financially.

At that time I was still managing my two health-food stores, my own health clinic, and was studying nutrition and oriental medicine. Sometimes I would even take tour groups across the country for a day. I was breast-feeding Yuval and raising Adi, not to mention caring for my husband, — a 35 year-old man who had spent the last year in a "big hole," so to speak. He would constantly speak negatively, refuse help, and was unable to work or cope with life.

I remembered the day when I'd had enough. I took the stick of a broom and made Danny get out of bed, because nothing could get him out of bed! But don't witches use brooms? And this cabalistic rabbi with his weird prescriptions wasn't that witchcraft?

******

"Happy birthday to you!" My mom burst into the room. "I have a wonderful present for you!" she said, handing me a carefully wrapped parcel.

Impatiently I unwrapped it. It was a book, *Dancing in the Light*, by Shirley MacLaine.

My mother had been a very "spiritual" lady for years. She practiced yoga and meditation periodically. She belonged to a highly organized "enlightened" group that met on every night of the full moon. At that time they would "send light" and expect the female leader of the group to hear the message given by spirit-beings called "the ascended masters." Mom was very advanced in these matters. Being a beautician and having her business at home, she had time to communicate her belief in the spirit world to as many as were open to listen.

I hadn't been open to this before, but now, I was ripe for some kind of spiritual revelation that would help explain my family situation and how I could cope.

******

"God, if this spiritual world exists, show it to me through a ouija board." I was kneeling beside my bed, praying fervently and straightforwardly. I was desperate. Shirley MacLaine seemed to have found her answers through "channeling." She was a respected actress and I wanted to know the truth.

Later on I would read a verse in the Bible that said;".... There shall not be found among you anyone who practices witchcraft or a soothsayer or one who interprets omens or a sorcerer or one who conjures spells or a medium or a spiritist or one who calls up the dead, for all who do these things are an abomination to the Lord..." (Deuteronomy 18:9-12). And; "You shall not suffer a sorceress to live," (Exodus 22:18). But at that time I was totally unaware of such warnings.

"Yes!"

Why was I getting involved with witchcraft, the devil and what is called in the Bible "the kingdom of darkness?" I was so ignorant. I didn't even know that astrology and numerology, and all such things, are linked with witchcraft and the occult and are strictly forbidden by God. At that time I just wanted to "touch reality."

It was only a few weeks later that a ouija board appeared in my life, in spite of the fact that there was not supposed to be any ouija boards in Israel as it was against the law. I had never seen one until shortly before I received one of my own.

This is what happened. After I had fallen on my knees and prayed for the Lord to reveal himself to me through a ouija board, a month or so passed. I did not tell anybody about this request. I just kept it between God and myself.

The manager of one of my business stores called me one day. She said, "Ronit, did you know that Michelle, (not her real name,) has a ouija board?" My manager didn't even know that I'd prayed for one!

As she said that, something snapped in me and I remembered my prayer. "Get me in touch with her," I told her.

"Well," she said, "she doesn't use it for just anybody. She's a medium. She only uses it for herself."

"Please," I told her, "put me in contact with her. She will receive me."

Although my manager gave me the telephone number, she actually called Michelle herself, and told her, "Ronit wants to have you minister to her with the ouija board."

Michelle answered, "Ronit? Oh, the spirits have already told me she would be calling. Of course. Yes! Tell her to come."

My manager was very happy about that. She called me back to say that Michelle would receive me.

"I knew it," I told her. "I knew she would!"

"Yes!"

The following day I drove my car to Michelle's apartment and went up to her place. We hugged each other. We really liked each other. She was the manager of the health club near my health food store and was a customer. In her apartment she showed me her ouija board and how to use it.

A few days later my other health food store manager, Sandy, decided to go to Canada to visit her family, for she was a Canadian Jewess.

Before she left I said "Sandy, please look for a ouija board in Canada and bring at least two of them for me."

"All right," she agreed.

She was gone for two weeks. When she came back, she brought one to me. "Ronit," she explained, "I went to a health food store and many places without finding one. Then I went to a toy shop, and there in the toy shop was a ouija board. It was the last one they had. It was also the last dollars that I had in my pocket! This is a miracle, because I was beginning to think I'd never find one for you, and I was almost out of money."

She handed me the ouija board and I took it to my house.

******

"Andrea," my mother said excitedly, "guess who has arrived in Israel and wants desperately to see you?"

I knew it! My heart was telling me all along that he would come any day. "It's Fred, isn't it?" (not his real name)

"Yes!" mom exclaimed. She had loved Fred as a son, but we hadn't seen him in 18 years!

Fred was my most beloved cousin. We had grown up together until our family left for Israel. We had loved one another as only children can love. When we played together, often he was the daddy and I the mommy and we would "take care of" my sisters and brother as if they were our children.

My heart was racing 200 miles an hour! This was exactly one year after Danny's birthday, when I had predicted that something terrible would happen if there was no change in Danny's situation. It was like a big change of destiny knocking on my door.

"Hola!" Fred called. With no more words, this handsome, tanned giant lifted me up in the air and gave me a "bear hug." He was strong, manly and real. His mixture of Argentinean and Spanish accent seemed delightful to me.

Our eyes interlocked in a long stare, as if we were inspecting each other's soul, trying to catch up with the 18 years of separation.

Chapter 11

Adultery

"Whoso commits adultery destroys his own soul" (Proverbs 6:32).

"If Danny ever cheats on me, I will castrate him!" I had said. When I was pregnant for the first time we had spent some days in Holland at the home of dear friends. They seemed very loose in "couple exchange," and I wanted them to understand my point of view about marital infidelity in no uncertain terms! I would not accept it. Period! My parents had given me an example of fidelity to one another, and I did not believe in that kind of freedom.

But Fred? That was something else! I was drowning. This was a "life-saver" for me. I even inquired of my "spirit-guides" from the ouija board, and they gave me all green lights.

My head was spinning. I was being loved as a woman after six years of rejection from my own husband. By this time, good friends had advised me to divorce Danny, since it was taking such a toll on me and his mental state was not getting any better. My answer had been, "I would not leave anybody on a sinking ship, let alone my husband!" I had been so optimistic! But now I was sinking myself.

"Danny," I said one day. "I know that you've noticed that something is happening between Fred and me."

He nodded despondently, yet with a flash of healthy jealousy in his eyes. "I want you to know," he said defiantly, "that if we divorce, I am taking the children with me. Over my dead body will you get them!"

This was the man whom I had been caring for like a baby! Now he was full of venomous fury. Later on I would read in the Song of Solomon in the Bible that "jealousy is as strong as death." This man, who had been insane and impotent for so long, was finally awakening to some normal feelings! Life is indeed strange.

"Please don't divorce me, Danny," I pleaded. "Give me time, just like I have given you time. This is stronger than me. Please wait for me!"

I was begging for grace from him, for I had reached the point of no return, and had absolutely no control over what was happening. I seemed to be in a whirlwind that was passing by and had happened to be caught in the midst of it. I was hopeless and helpless.

And all the time these "spirit-guides" were giving me hope and direction. I was no longer able to see that all their instructions were contrary to my beliefs. They were leading me on a very fast road of destruction. Right and wrong had no meaning any more. Discipline and responsibility were labeled as "square" and cumbersome. My head was buzzing and spinning.

Was I losing my mind?

******

"Here," I said hurriedly and impatiently, handing a very confused note to one of my health-food store managers. On this note I had written the most deranged message I would ever write. It said:

"Yes!"

Shalom. I am leaving with my lover to Eilat. I have found the meaning of life. Take care of the store and don't worry about me.

This was the 7th of April, 1988, the very day which the "spirit-guides" had instructed me to leave the area in order to establish myself as their tool in the "liberal" city of Eilat on the Red Sea.

The children of Israel crossed the Red Sea when they were released from slavery by God through Moses. I was going in a totally opposite direction! I had willingly and ignorantly enslaved myself to the devil through a ouija board.

A few days earlier I had been in a Yoga Retreat. Later, Danny came to pick me up to take me home. He smelled good. He had shaved and dressed up to the best of his ability. This situation had caused him to sober up miraculously!

"Here," he said humbly and in a broken tone. "I brought some flowers for you."

I hardened myself. What is he trying to do, I said to myself. He hasn't brought me flowers in years!

Out loud I said, "Thank you," forcing a smile and trying not to betray my thoughts. He seemed to be softer than I had ever seen him. He was desperately trying to win me over as a woman and a wife. Inside, my heart was breaking. I had never seen him so real, so vulnerable. He seemed truly repentant.

But yoga had taught me control over my emotions and not to allow circumstances to affect me. I hardened my heart toward him. My heart had finally become a heart of stone.

******

"We'll be landing in Eilat in ten minutes," the melodious voice of the Hebrew-speaking stewardess announced.

I buckled my seat belt and put out my cigarette. I was dressed in pink and yellow and looked like a cone full of creamy ice cream, ready to meet Fred. He would be waiting for me at the airport and we would spend some time pursuing "the things of the spirit" together.

On the other side of Israel an 18-month old baby boy was crying, and there was no mommy to comfort him. "Where has mommy gone?" he would ask, again and again.

A nearly five-year-old girl was sitting on the corner of her bed, her heart tight with dread and her eyes filled with tears. "What has happened to mommy?"

The plane was landing and my head was spinning. "I'm going to see him again." My heart was beating fast with great expectancy mixed with an unexpected hint of fear and insecurity... "And what if he is not waiting for me?" "I have left everything to follow him," I thought to myself, walking down the aircraft stairs. "And what if he backs off and leaves me?" As these thoughts were roaming through my mind I discerned a big tall, dark man with long hair in the waiting hall...But why was he pacing to and fro instead of running to meet me? And why did he seem so worried? What was he muttering to himself? Could it be that he wants to back off?.... O God!....."Hi!" I was standing next to him and he hadn't noticed..."O, you are here," he said with a forced smile, or did I imagine it? "You look very nice," he continued with the same tone of voice. "Come on let's go!"

"Hello?" Fred held the telephone tightly. "How is she? What? When? The funeral tomorrow at 1 p.m? I'll be there!"

Fred was white when he turned to me. Auntie Juanita had died and we were required to go to her funeral the following day. Being cousins, of course we shared the same family, the same mourning.

We rented a car and I drove us all the way back to Tel Aviv in five hours.

"Yes!"

Fred was very tense. All the family would be gathered there, and what everyone had known about us through rumors would be exposed.

Chapter 12

Demonic Freedom

I was beginning to miss my children very much. Before returning to Eilat, one day, when I was able to see my daughter I asked her, "Adi, how would you like to come with mommy to Eilat?"

"Yes!" she cried, clapping her hands in delight.

Without telling anyone, I took her back to Eilat with me.

Danny traced us, found the hotel where we were staying, "rescued" her and took her home with him. I was alone again!

******

I began rebelling against the instruction of my spirit-guides. In one of these outbursts of rebellion I flew back to Tel Aviv to try to see my children again. My mother's heart was waking up to the painful reality that I missed my children. No spirits in the world could keep me away from them!

"Hello? Anybody here?" I called. I was longing to see my children! A friend had come with me from Eilat, and was waiting for me in the car.

"Take them in! Quick! Cover their eyes! Don't let them see her! She's crazy!" Danny shouted.

Danny's brother got out of a car and punched me as if we were in a boxing match, to knock me down. Danny's violence and fury rose, and he kicked me violently into the car of my shocked friend.

I was completely bruised and shocked. I ended the day by seeing a gynecologist who checked me, to make sure that I could still give birth, for I was badly hurt.

******

"You can come with us voluntarily, or we will take you by force," they said.

The men of Danny's family and my step-sister, five people in all, grabbed me by force, totally against my will and put me in their car. Before I could grasp what was going on, I was being checked into the regional mental hospital. I was taken in, and I heard the door distinctly locking behind me.

A male nurse approached me with a big smile. "Here, Sweetheart," he said, "I've brought you these pajamas. You can change in Adis' room."

I glared at him with a most frightening look, until he slowly backed off and left me alone with my grief, still wearing my expensive business dress.

I refused to eat, and paced around like a lioness in a cage. Then all of a sudden it dawned on me. There were bars on all the windows! This place was completely fortified! I grabbed one of the bars as if wanting to pull them out from the window and stuck my nose out. Lo and behold, there were roses outside, and I couldn't even smell them from in here!

"Yes!"

A lady screamed in agony. In a few moments she was dead silent. She had received an effective shot for her nerves. No comfort, just syringes.

******

I saw his back, and his dark complexion. Danny was here again. He was leaning on the counter, almost breathing on the receptionist, making sure —. "Don't let her out too quick," he said forcefully. "She's dangerous! Don't believe a thing she says! She will trick you. She is a good actress. Don't let her go!" He was being pushy, full of venom mixed with desperation.

"Sir," the receptionist said firmly, finally losing her patience, "we know how to conduct our business in here!" With determined elegance, she opened the heavy front door and motioned him out.

Something in my heart was breaking. Though demon-possessed to the core, I could still recognized that this was the man I had loved, nurtured, cared for and even provided for. This man — whom I had loved more than myself — this man whom I had refused to commit to an institution when his mental condition was unbearable, was now bringing destruction upon me and our entire family. This same man! He had been standing there making sure I would not be released. He was full of poison and bitterness because of the way things had turned out.

That really broke whatever was healthy in my heart! From that time on, all my natural defense mechanisms were broken. Now I was totally at the mercy of the demonic spirits. Part of my soul had crumbled to pieces, and thus I remained, until the time came when the One called "the Lover of my soul" would put it back together again, by the power of true Love.

******

Three days later I held in my hand a most invaluable document. It was "A letter of sanity." For the last three days I had been interviewed by five psychiatrists, one social worker and one kind lady psychologist. They had turned me "inside out" and probed into my innermost being, asking me the most wounding questions in scientific language.

Since I was a nutrition and health consultant, I answered them in the same "lingo" and kept them all busy doing some intellectual exercises.

"Come on," they said, "be reasonable. Just sign this document, and you can stay here and rest for fifteen days. You really need a rest!"

Seven pairs of eyes were staring at me, trying to find my weak points. I crossed my legs in a business-type fashion and replied with determination that I would not. "If I wanted a rest, I would have chosen the Swiss Alps and not this place." I refused to sign anything.

The psychologist, who was the only one showing kindness, had favored me and produced a very good report. "She is somewhat excitable, but I see no signs of mental illness," her report said.

Ha! I had played their game right. Every time they asked me about spiritual things I just gave a flat and boring answer, as if the spiritual realm didn't exist at all.

"Oh, I'm happy to see you out!"
That was number 1.
"What a surprise! You are out already!"
That was number 2.
"Here you are, out and ready to go!"
That was number 3.
"Have you been released? Well, I'm happy for you."
That was number 4.
A few more minutes went by, and then finally,

"Yes!"

"Aren't you —? Yes, you are. And out so soon! How wonderful!" Yes, that was number 5.

All five psychiatrists had congratulated me for being "out," released from the "cuckoo's nest"!

A few hours earlier I had been standing in front of a very astonished social worker. "If you don't let me leave today as you promised, I will sue you!" I said. "You are keeping me here against the law, as I have not signed any document agreeing to my confinement. Open that door and let me out!"

"But Mrs. F.," she said anxiously, "the doctor hasn't come yet. The moment he comes in, we'll call you."

"No!" I said. I was very annoyed! "You told me the same thing yesterday. The psychologist's report said I was not mentally ill. Therefore I have no business being here. You let me out now, or this whole hospital will regret this!" I meant business, and I knew my lawyer would fight with me, and for me.

As by an act of divine intervention — they let me go free!

Later on I received the painful but sobering revelation that Danny had not been the only one involved in this forced confinement. Actually, the main instigator against me had been my own mother - the one who had given me that infamous book by Shirley MacLaine which triggered my walk down the dark path of the occult. She had now helped to engineer to have me put away in a mental hospital, just as I had suspected, she had done to my brother eight years earlier!

For all those eight years he had wandered through many different institutions and had taken many different drugs, never finding true freedom for his soul and his spirit.

It was my own mother who conspired in having my children taken away from me, and having me confined. I felt that there was no compassion in her to help me in my time of need. It was as it had been when as a child, I had learned to hide all emotions and weaknesses from her, for it seemed to lead only to cruelty.

Later, from the Bible, I read that one of the curses that could come on a family because of involvement in the occult is, and was, and will be, mental illness and insanity. This includes involvement in any type of magic, astrology, witchcraft, meditation, divination, contacting any spirits, (other than the Spirit of God), calling upon the dead, palm reading, yoga, (calling upon other gods), and channeling of any sort. My dear mom had been a pioneer in nearly all of these for many years.

My ancestors as rabbis had been into kabbalism, which really is a Jewish occult practice. My paternal grandfather used to be a "master freemason," which is a most hideous and deceptive form of devil worship, disguised as "good works" and "morality." My parents were proud of such ancestry.

Later on the Bible told me that the curses of the forefathers are visited on their children up to the fourth generation. My brother had paid for this ancestry by losing his mind. The demons were after me to do the same.

******

A very familiar car was following me closely. I was walking briskly with adamant determination. "They will not force me to stay here," I said to myself. "I am going back to Eilat!"

The red car continued to follow me persistently. The demon spirits hissed in my ears, making my head buzz. I had gone through so much in the last month! I had become psychic, and I needed no ouija board to communicate with the spirit-guides any more. I had become a ouija board to myself.

I was totally possessed and controlled by these beings that continually told me of their "love" for me. I was not my own. I knew that "somebody" was inhabiting me but I could not discern anymore who I was and who "they", (the spirit-guides,) were. I had no feelings. I was totally numb to reality.

"Come into the car," called the very familiar voice of the driver. "Your children miss you!"

My two children were sitting inside with expectant and bewildered eyes. A spark of humanity and forgotten motherly instinct crossed through my heart as a piercing needle — only to be suffocated by spiritual voices that were numbing my emotions.

Nevertheless, like an automaton I opened the door of the car and joined my family, to Danny's great relief.

******

Danny had left me all alone in his parents' house with Adi. I had managed to trick him into thinking that I had become normal again. But I had just received fresh instructions from the "inhabitants" controlling my will and emotions.

"Adi," I said, "we're going. Shhhh! You will see. I have a surprise for you!"

"Mommie," Adi said, looking out of the small plane window, "is that Eilat down there?"

Poor baby. She was so confused, and yet she was trying to maintain sanity, even trying to enjoy the situation.

I had left our car in a mess, at the airport at Tel Aviv, as I hurriedly boarded the plane with my precious cargo, my kidnapped daughter.

Danny had not wanted to give me the children. He had said, "Over my dead body!"

Then I'll just have to take them, I had thought. Why was my head buzzing all the time?

"Yes!"

It was 4 o'clock in the morning and I was dancing again. I was a real attraction. My head tied in colorful scarves, with heavy makeup, tight jeans, or free-flowing scarves for skirts, I was a picture to behold!

I had managed to kidnap Adi through a private detective. This time I had the police of Eilat on my side, as Danny had threatened to kill me. The man was desperate, and rightly so. Yet how was it that he was now so sober and so rational, after being out of his mind for more than a year?

Then I remembered my prayer of many months before: "God, if you are real, heal my husband!"

God was real then, but was this that I was experiencing also from God?

"Adi," I said, "pass me the cards, and watch what Mommy does."

I was reading palms and cards intuitively. I had never studied it. These demons gave me power and divination as part of the deal.

Adi was learning, in spite of herself, some things that later on I would have to work hard to cleanse from her mind and her memories.

Chapter 13

Light, Where Are You Lost?

I woke up, startled. I was being called. "Dominique! Dominique!"

I knew that was my name, but where did I get it? It sounded good to me, but I could not explain how my name had changed overnight!

I went to the citizen's bureau in Eilat and changed my name officially. I was no longer Andrea. From now on I would be known as Dominique the dancer.

Many doors opened for me to dance. One of them was in the casino boat.

"Look at her," said the heavyset, coarse multi-millionaire to one of his body guards. "She seems to have psychic powers. Every number that she gambles on, wins."

I was piling up money. My demonic spirit-guides knew how to gamble and also knew how to manipulate the game. Soon I became a threat to the casino boat and they threw me out.

After my hospital episode, my heart had completely hardened. I had desensitized myself down to the soles of my feet, as though walking on hard stones. Life wasn't so bad after all!

"*Yes!*"

"Mommy, look what I can do!" Adi was having fun in the swimming pool of the hotel where I was working as a hostess and entertainer.

It was hot. August in Eilat is like a living hell where all those who have rejected God will burn forever. Hot, hot, very hot! But Adi was enjoying this place, and that made me very happy.

"He's coming after you! He said that he will kill you! Just wait and see what he will do to you!" These fears haunted me day and night. I knew that Danny had found me, for he had called my boss at the club hotel and had said the most terrible things about me.

I was afraid. I knew that if he'd take Adi from me again, I would die. Loving her was the only thing that kept me alive. Yuval my son was beyond my reach, yet the private detective had managed to get Adi to me through an ingenious plan. Danny had already sued me for divorce and we had been in court together a few months earlier.

Still fresh in my mind was the way I had escaped from court, because he had a lawyer and I had none. I had run away from the court. A sweet, compassionate lawyer found me and decided to plead my case free of charge, until I could be back on my feet.

"Mommy, I'm hungry!" Adi called, interrupting my thoughts. She was all wet, sun-tanned and beautiful.

"Let's go eat," I said, grabbing her hand.

******

"Yes, Shmuel. I understand. We will be back then. Yes, soon, —." I was talking to my lawyer.

He had advised me to return to my home area, get a decent job, start taking care of whatever was left of my business, and to continue fighting for the custody of my children.

"Yes!"

We had a good case. I had a document proving that I was sane. There was proof that Danny had been manic-depressive. There were witnesses. The children were small enough for the rabbis in the rabbinical, (religious), court to side with me.

I was being sued for divorce on the biblical grounds of adultery.

******

Adi was fast asleep with her little head on my lap. I was so exhausted that I could barely make one more decision.

"Here we are, Ma'am. We have arrived in Raanana." The driver had been very compassionate during the five hours it had taken us to drive back from Eilat. He had sensed that I was totally broken, and had been very sweet with me.

He helped me with my suitcases, and I grabbed Adi, taking her by the hand. It was six o'clock in the morning and the neighborhood was peaceful.

I was coming back like a prodigal, after four months of deep devastation. My mom opened the door with a troubled look on her face, and motioned us in.

Even though I was grateful to be back, the spiritual atmosphere in my parents' home was far from healthy. My mom was so involved in the spiritual-demonic, thinking that it was different from what I had been doing. It was more organized, and thus looked cleaner. I found myself fighting with more demonic opposition, for familiar spirits were all around. My dad was fighting a destructive cancer, and his body was rapidly changing.

"Here, Daddy," I said with tenderness to my sick father. "I want you to eat this. You will feel better."

My dad trusted me in health matters and accepted my instructions. He began to feel better even though we had only been back for a week, for I had been pouring love and care on him.

"Andrea," my mom said, "Would you allow Adi to go with Natalia to her kibbutz?" Natalia was my step-sister, the one that had helped to put me in the mental institution. She had been adopted into our family, after we had met her in Mexico. Rejected by her own family, my mom and dad had decided to be parents to her. We all loved her and admired her strength of character and intelligence, as she overcame the misfortunes in her life. Yet, Nat, (as we called her,) was a really needy young woman, needy for God and for true emotional healing, that only a personal encounter with Him could bring. "It would be really healing for her," mom said, "to see nature and visit the cows and sheep. That way you could have a rest."

The suggestion sounded good to me and I was exhausted. Adi and I had been hiding in my mom's house so that Danny couldn't come and take Adi from me by force.

Little did I know that this was a plot between Danny and my mother, for Danny to take my daughter back.

Ahhhhh! Mommy! Mommy! How could I have trusted you!

****

From the second floor of my health food store I had a much better view of the disaster. The air-conditioning was still there. The electronic scales were still intact. There were some dried fruits and herbs left. But oh, was the place dirty!

My biggest shop looked as if someone had deserted it in a hurry after a hurricane had hit town! Four months earlier, I had deserted my business, led by my spirit-guides. Now, I had come back to see what was left of my life.

As I saw the amazing neglect and devastation in the store, I realized I was looking at a vivid picture of my own life and soul. A wreck! And in only four months! I was awaking from an unbelievable nightmare. Was this all real?

Adi had been taken back. I had been betrayed. My store was destroyed. I had sold my other store in the heat of insanity. My reputation had been ruined. It was as though my soul had been snatched from me. I was physically exhausted.

With the last of the will power I had left, in a determined act, I grabbed all the crayons that I had and scratched on a piece of paper these peculiar words:

"Light, where are you lost? Come to me!"

As I was writing that with fury, one of my spirit-guides tried to tie my hands and arms, desperately fighting against my determination.

And all this started while reading the book, *Dancing in the Light*, by Shirley MacLaine.

So where was the light lost???

Chapter 14

The Light Of The World

All dressed up in my favorite pink dress, I looked so stunning that it made heads turn. Actually, I was a type of Mary Magdalene, that famous harlot who repented and devoted her life to serving the Jewish Messiah, Yeshua (Jesus), after he cast seven demons out of her.

I was walking with a seductive yet despondent pace down Ben Yehuda street in Tel Aviv.

"Shalom. I'm pleased to meet you. My name is Benny (not his real name), and I am a tour guide."

He was tall, handsome and a distinctive-looking gentleman, but I was furious with anyone of the male gender and would not open to more encounters.

I was about to answer abruptly when the words "tour guide" hit my benumbed brain. Wasn't I a tour guide, too? Like a well-programmed robot, I extended my hand to him and said, "Shalom! My name is Dominique and I am a tour guide, too."

He was elated and pleasantly surprised. "Would you happen to be a tour guide in Spanish?"

"Yes," I said, "Spanish, French, English, Hebrew. You can choose."

"Wonderful! Wonderful! What a coincidence! Well, well. As a matter of fact, I am right now searching for a Spanish tour guide to work with me on a private tour for of some lovely Mexican people. Would you take the job?"

A few thoughts went through my mind. I wasn't all together. I was exhausted. Life had no meaning anymore. I was penniless and in debt, but I had nothing to lose and it might even be refreshing to be normal again.

"Okay," I said. "When do we start?"

One layer of make-up won't do, I said to myself. I'll have to hide all of these sores. What a disgrace!

My skin had broken out in the most terrible blisters as a result of the distresses of the last four and a half months. My skin used to be my number one calling card, and now I needed three or four layers of make-up to look halfway decent.

A few days before, I had found myself at a "spiritual" party, which one of my dear friends had invited me to. She was an expert in the cultic practice of bio-energy. Astar was really trying to help me overcome the tragic episode of my last few months. It was "the blind leading the blind," as she desperately needed assistance also, for her "spiritual forces" were ruining her own life.

I was dancing in a trance, concentrating on bringing my soul back into my body. Astar said, "Do some 'grounding,' in order to cause your soul to return."

I was desperate, as I felt like an empty body with no soul. It was the most nauseating thing I have ever experienced. My soul was literally gone! Someone, or something, had stolen it from me.

All of a sudden, as I was lying on the ground doing the 'grounding,' I felt part of my soul had returned from captivity. As I looked up I saw a man with compassionate dove's eyes sitting there. He was different from all the rest, and was looking right at me.

"I have seen your suffering," he said, "and I prayed to God for you."

Was he an angel? Was this man real? He didn't seem to know anyone there, and he didn't seem to fit into this place. Whether he was an angel, or a man, someone had heard his prayers!

******

"Shalom! Bienvenidos a la Tierra Santa," I said, greeting my tiny Mexican group in Spanish with the words, "Welcome to the Holy Land." "We will be leaving for Galilee the first thing in the morning," I told them.

They looked happy, very expectant, and full of humor. How refreshing they were! There were eight people in all. These people were fun to be with! They were devoted Catholics, and among the eight, two were priests. One was an old priest, a holy man who had spent most of his life in prayer and seclusion, studying and meditating upon the word of God.

The other was a young priest who said he was willing to quit his priesthood, if I'd marry him. He was joking, of course. This was going to be a good time!

******

"No," said the elderly priest, "you join us during the Mass and sit right here with the priests. You are like a shepherdess."

I was flattered and intrigued. I had seen many Masses, but I didn't remember ever having partaken of a full service before.

My tour guide friend who had given me this job was doing all the driving. He caught a glimpse of me joining these Catholics in their worship, and his eyes opened wide.

A Jewess partaking of a Catholic Mass? Yet, he did not judge or stop me.

The music and joyous singing had started. "We worship you, Jesus, Savior..." I sang along with them. It was fun, and besides, it made me feel good for the first time in quite a while.

"No! No! No!" I was violently resisting this power that was trying to put me on my knees before the Cross just after we had finished the service.

"Here, honey. Let me help you." A sweet lady from the group helped me down to my knees. I couldn't resist this power any more!

I didn't want any more spirits. I wanted to be free! But this one was different. It was powerful, yet gentle; determined, yet forceful. I yielded, surrendering to the strong yet gentle embrace of the Spirit of God.

There I was, kneeling in front of the cross of a man known to me as Jesus Christ. Perplexed due to my being Jewish, I heard the voice of the Almighty God speaking to my heart. "Run for your life!" the voice said "Be baptized, and be saved!" That very same day as we were driving with the tour group back to Jerusalem, the older priest came to me and told me this: "Your name is Dominiquae, because the addition of the Latin suffix "ae" means that you belong to God!"

Chapter 15

Yes!

This is certainly your last card, my thoughts told me. Run, young woman! Run, or die, for the Light is passing by!
Where do I run for my life? — I've got to run! — O God, help me! — Who can help me? — How do I get baptized? — I want to be saved. I need to be saved. — I'm dying! — O God, help!!

"I want to see him. No, I have not made an appointment. Lady, this is a life or death situation! I have got to meet him t0day!"

I was forceful and desperate. This was the headquarters of The Christian Embassy in Jerusalem. As a tour guide, I was well acquainted with the place. I was demanding to meet with the leader.

"Come follow me," said the secretary. "He will join you in a minute."

I was nervous, excited and compulsive.

"Shalom, young lady. How can I help you?"

He looked tall and threatening, yet his loving voice soothed my nerves and I proceeded to explain to him what had happened to me by the Sea of Galilee. "And now please find me a Catholic, Franciscan church and baptize me, immediately!" I said, concluding my story.

He smiled slightly and said, "No, no, no. You will never stop being Jewish. You have to remain Jewish and serve the Lord. I cannot give you my blessing to convert to Catholicism. Here is the telephone number of some Jewish people who have found their Messiah. They will help you."

I was indignant! Wasn't he supposed to proselytize me? But here he was, turning me back to my own Jewish religion! And what was this whole business of a "Jewish Messiah?" What on earth did Jesus or Christianity have to do with being Jewish, or finding the Jewish Messiah?

I felt betrayed by the Christian Embassy! I left, irritated and disappointed, crumpling the note in my hand. All that was on it was a name, and the telephone number of other Jews like me.

It was the beginning of September, 1988 and it was still hot. In the shade of the tiny apartment I had rented in Jerusalem, I managed to cool down, both physically and emotionally.

Okay, I said to myself, I can call these Messianic Jews. What can I lose anyway? And perhaps, after all, the Christian ambassador knew what he was doing.

I picked up the phone. "Shalom," I said, "may I speak with Batya?"

"Speaking," said the melodious voice at the other end of the line. We talked for a few minutes, and she invited me to come to a special Sunday meeting at 7:00 p.m. at the Y.M.C.A. building. "You will like it," she told me.

******

"The court will rise." The rabbinical judge came in and motioned for the opening of the court case;

"F. versus F."

Danny looked so serious, ready to explode at any minute! His lawyer had trouble keeping him calm.

"Yes!"

My lawyer had deserted me. He said I was out of my mind because I had decided to quit fighting. I had this inner peace that I had to give up everything - children, car, even my underwear if necessary!

I was exhausted from all the striving and fighting. My wrist was still wounded from the last encounter with Danny. He had brought the children over to my apartment in Jerusalem so I could spend my first weekend with them after months of separation.

One thing had led to another, and before I knew it Danny was furiously beating me in front of the children. He twisted my wrist so badly that I almost passed out and the children were in shock. My heart was torn that my children had witnessed that! I knew one thing. I'd rather die than have the children watch scenes like this again. Danny was constantly threatening to kill me, constantly telling me how everyone hated me. No, I was not going to fight anymore!

When I had ended up in the hospital due to the injury to my wrist, I had managed to overcome the trauma, thanks to the loving intervention and support of Tammy and Avner, dear, faithful friends of mine. But on that day I had decided that I should divorce Danny and give up the children.

"Where is your lawyer, ma'am?" The voice of the judge brought my mind back to the courtroom.

"I have no lawyer."

The judge looked puzzled. It didn't look like a fair game to him, and it wasn't. "Your husband is accusing you of adultery. Do you plead guilty?"

"Yes, your honor. I am guilty."

"What is the agreement concerning the children?"

Danny's lawyer answered. "The mother has agreed to relinquish custody of the children to the father." His words felt like a death sentence to my heart!

The judge turned to me. "But aren't the children very young?"

"Yes, your Honor," replied Danny's lawyer. "The boy is two, and the girl five."

The rabbi-judge turned to me again, very perplexed that I had voluntarily given up my children who were so young.

The threatening voice of Danny was echoing in my mind: "Over my dead body will you get the children! I will kill you if it is necessary!"

Why was my wrist hurting so much? The rabbi knew, in his heart of hearts, that this young, broken woman loved her children enough, — yes, even enough to give them up!

The rabbi-judge looked at me with eyes of compassion and sympathy. "This is not right," he said. "You have no lawyer, and you are all alone."

"Your honor," I replied with a sudden burst of dignity, — yes, and hope. "God is my lawyer! God is my Judge, and he will bring me back my children in His own timing!"

******

"Flight 324 to Lisbon, Portugal will be leaving in 15 minutes," came the announcement.

"Shalom," I said to my tourists. "It's time for you to go. The plane will be leaving soon. They hugged me warmly and disappeared into the crowd.

It had been a successful tour. For the first time in my life, I had guided in Portuguese, and I don't even know Portuguese! It's exciting how "necessity becomes the mother of invention."

It was 4 o'clock in the morning. The Ben Gurion airport in Tel Aviv was busy, and I was one very exhausted tour guide heading for a taxi to take me home to Jerusalem.

"Hallelujah, Praise the Lord!" Before I knew it I was sandwiched into a taxi, between two rejoicing Christian "giants." They were so happy.

"Hello, sister," they said, "let's sing." And they began, "Rejoice in the Lord always, and again I say, rejoice! Rejoice! Rejoice!..."

I sang with them. The car was traveling smoothly along the Israeli highway to Jerusalem, as if carried by the sounds of the song we were singing.

"Louise," I said to the red-headed Christian girl sitting next to me, "what sign of the horoscope are you?"

She looked at me indignantly. "I am not a sign in the horoscope. I am a born again Christian."

Born again. Born again. What does "born again" mean?

I sneaked in. It was past 7:00 p.m. An usher motioned me to a seat in the center of the spacious auditorium at the Y.M.C.A.. building on King David Street. This was the "special meeting" Batya had told me about, that she had said I would like. I could see the screen pretty well.

"Emmanuel, Emmanuel. God with us, revealed in us. Your name is called, Emmanuel," they all sang.

How pretty, I said to myself. There is such an atmosphere of harmony and love and yes, peace, here.

"He is the King of kings," they sang. "He is the Lord of lords. His name is Jesus, Jesus, Jesus, Oooooohhh —. He is the King!"

Yes, I was growing to love that name — Jesus. "Hineh, Yeshua, Yeshuat Yisrael, hineh hu, hallelu....[Here is Yeshua, the salvation of Israel. Here he is. Praise him!]"

They were singing in Hebrew, and using a strange name, Yeshua, instead of Jesus. Was Yeshua, Jesus?

"If you are in need of prayer, come forward and we will pray for you," the pastor announced.

What does that mean? I thought to myself. I never heard of being prayed for in this way. But before I knew it, I felt as if an expert puppeteer had pulled my strings and I found myself walking down the aisle leading to the prayer line forming before the altar.

One of the ministers was praying loudly: "In Jesus name, devil, I command you to leave this man!"

That terrified me! God, I said in my heart, if you are here, please send somebody quiet to pray for me! I was afraid enough to run away! I am Jewish, I thought. What am I doing here???

"What can I pray for you, sister?" asked the quiet, gentle voice of a kind-looking man.

"I — I — I." I didn't know what to say! Then I said, "I am Jewish and I feel as if I'm the only Jewish person in Israel who loves Jesus."

He smiled warmly and said, "I am Jewish too, and there are many more across the country who have discovered Yeshua as the true Jewish Messiah."

What a comfort! I wasn't the only one!

"Now," he said, going straight to business. "Have you given Yeshua your life and your heart?"

I didn't know what he was asking. It sounded like Chinese to me! Yet my heart leaped within me and I quickly said, "Yes!"

I had to say yes. It was either yes or die! I didn't know exactly what I had said yes to. Yet I knew Whom I had said yes to: to God, as represented by his Son, Jesus, Yeshua, the Messiah of Israel and the Savior of the world.

When I left the meeting that night, I was not the same. My heart had gone through a supernatural experience. I had been born again!!

Chapter 16

Born Again, Baby Steps

"There is sunshine in my heart today. La, la la la, la la la!" Happiness had come into my heart. My heart was able to sing! The sorrow and deep grief of the last few months was lifting.

I lit a cigarette. — What was happening here? I felt as if there was Someone in the room taking my cigarette away! I resisted at first, but then gave in. This Somebody seemed to love me and care for me.

Then this spiritual "Somebody" prompted me to go to the kitchen, open the refrigerator and grab a stack of contraceptive pills. Along with my cigarettes and pills, this spirit guide from God led me to the garbage container and led me to throw out all this unholy booty.

As soon as I had done that, I felt so free! I was never to smoke again or to commit sexual immorality. I began singing, "I have decided to follow Jesus,...no turning back, no turning back."

But who or what was this spiritual presence that had caused me to dump all these things?

******

"Yes!"

It was around 10 o'clock in the morning and my tiny flat was a mess. I had been working in tourism, guiding one group after another and everything seemed to be happening. Jesus had come into my life and it was changing. Yet my heart was broken because of my children, my marriage, my stores and all.

"I'm lonely," I sighed. I was 29, and now had to start all over again with so many scars, no family to help and no friends. Just then the telephone rang, as if someone had been reading my mind!

"Hello, Shalom. Yes, I remember you. You are the tall, red-headed fellow that I met at the airport when you joined the taxi I was taking back to Jerusalem."

"You have a good memory," Larry, (not real name,) replied with a joyful voice. "I wonder if you would like to have a cup of coffee with me, and then join me as I sing at the Hebrew Union College. Christians and reformed Jews are meeting today, to fellowship."

My heart said yes, so I replied, "Okay. What time?"

"Open to the book of Jeremiah," Larry said to me.

I opened the Bible I had received as a present at a tourist store in Bethlehem.

"Chapter 31, verse 31. Read, Dominiquae!"

I opened my mouth and slowly and deliberately read the verse aloud: "The day will come says the Lord, when I will make a new covenant with the people of Israel and Judah."

This was good stuff! I was getting excited! "Can I read the next verse too?" I asked, eager to continue.

"Sure," he replied with a big grin on his face.

And I read: "It won't be like the one I made with their fathers when I took them by the hand to bring them out of the land of Egypt — a covenant they broke, even though I was a husband to them, says the Lord."

"Larry," I asked, "then have I entered into the new covenant with the God of Israel?"

"Yes, my little sister," he said. "When you accepted Jesus' blood to atone for your sins, and you decided to surrender to him and follow him, you experienced something in your heart, didn't you?"

"Did I! Yes, it was the most interesting experience," I said, "even though I didn't fully understand what happened."

"Why," he said, "you became a new creation. You were born again as you entered into new covenant with God, by your faith and acceptance of Jesus Christ, whose birth name in Hebrew is Yeshua."

I took a deep breath. We were seated at a beautiful cafe overlooking the Citadel and the walls of Jerusalem. The lights of Jerusalem surrounded us as a band of angels.

"Let's go for a walk," he said.

"So, what is 'a new creation'?" I asked, trying to figure it all out.

"Here." He opened his Bible to 2 Corinthians 5:17, "read for yourself."

"Therefore if anyone is in Christ, (which means Messiah)," I read, "he is a new creation. The old has gone, the new has come."

The new has come, I thought to myself. The old has gone. I needed this!

Larry looked at me with a strange look. "Dominiquae," he asked, "have you received the baptism in the Holy Spirit?"

"No!" I said, emphatically and defensively. "Jesus, yes. Spirits, no!!" He couldn't possibly understand what I had gone through! He could not guess why I hated that word "spirit" with a passion. And I couldn't explain it.

He laughed. We were sitting on a bench at the top of the hill, looking towards the walls of old Jerusalem again. He boldly placed his arm around me. I cringed, because it took me by surprise.

Then he prayed aloud, "Abba, Father, I thank you for giving Dominiquae the baptism in the Holy Spirit, with the evidence of speaking in other tongues."

As Larry was praying I felt embraced by a force that caused me to quiet down. I was surrounded by the sweetest sensation! And a Voice inside me said, "First go home and burn the drawing of the ouija board that you did."

I stopped Larry abruptly. "I know what to do," I said, and added without further explanation, "I have to go home immediately and do something, and then I will receive."

I wasn't afraid anymore. The Lord had given me his peace and his instruction. I proceeded to follow it faithfully and without delay. I boarded the bus home and waved Larry goodbye.

"Burn!" I commanded this unholy paper. "Burn!" echoed my soul and every inch of my being. "Oh, how I hated what this represented — ouija board, witchcraft, destruction, lies, loss, pain, suffering, immorality, my death, and the death of many others involved in it, thinking it was fun, or spiritual, or harmless. I hate you, devil, cried my heart with a passion."

The drawing was burning steadily on the top of my sink. I watched intently, in total concentration as every bit of it was being eaten by the flames, along with my tragic past.

I sighed with relief. Wooh! — A powerful gush of wind put me on my knees. Waves of fluid air or fresh spiritual waters washed over my soul and every corner of my being. Out of my mouth came the most melodious languages I had ever spoken!

My heart started crying out to God in repentance for all the evil things I had done. The dam of my eyes and my heart broke, and I began crying buckets of tears of repentance and relief.

Waves upon waves of the Holy Spirit filled me, loved me, washed me, and talked to me. I prayed in many different tongues, some of them known languages, some of them unknown, which the Bible calls "tongues of angels."

Five hours later, at 5 in the morning I rose from the hard, cold concrete floor, without a single mark on my knees, and with a totally new soul, new strength. I was light as a feather, filled with the power of God and his joy and faith — never to be the same again!

I felt forgiven and cleansed, and knew that I was a new creation. The old had gone and the new had come!

Chapter 17

Empowered By The Spirit

"I can do all things through Jesus Christ who gives me strength." I quoted this verse often to myself while I was trying to overcome so much. My body and my soul were still bearing fresh marks of the occult. The only strength that I had in my daily life was the strength that the Spirit of God gave me as I prayed, obeying his word and worshipping him. I soon realized that without relying on the power of the Holy Spirit I wouldn't make it. I sensed a raging war going on in the heavenlies, as the devil was sending hosts of spirit-demons to cause me to fall. The war was intense and very tangible.

One day I was boarding a bus that would take me to my destination in Jerusalem, when all of a sudden a dark force pressed against my head and attacked my body. I stumbled, and fell almost unconscious on one of the seats.

"I recognize you," I said, grinding my teeth and trying to breathe. "I bind you, devil, in Jesus' name and I command you to leave me!"

I was nauseous and beaten, gasping for air, yet at the sound of my command "In Jesus name," the dark force lifted and left me!

******

"Do you know what you are doing?" asked Larry, before immersing me into the Sea of Galilee.

I took a quick glimpse at my two beautiful children playing peacefully on the beach and quickly answered. "Yes. And these two children, Adi and Yuval, will be my witnesses."

In the name of Jesus," Larry intoned, "I proclaim that as a token of obedience to your faith in Jesus the Messiah of Israel, representing his death, burial and resurrection, I baptize you this day!"

I went into the water and came out with outstretched arms to heaven and shouts of joy. "Halleluiah! Praise the Lord!"

Adi and Yuval watched and smiled. "Mommy," Adi said, "when are we going to eat?"

******

"All of it," I said to Larry. "I want you to inspect all of it and throw out everything that does not give glory to God in this place."

"Well," he answered, "most of your books are new age or occult or yoga and witchcraft. So they all have to go." He was talking about hundreds of dollars worth of books, spiritual books that I used to love.

"Go ahead," I told him. "Enjoy yourself. I trust that you will do a better job than I would. You have been walking with God longer than I have. I trust you."

Piles of books went into the trash that day. The dancing garments that I had used to dance in bars were also thrown out. My little apartment was being emptied from unholy, cursed influences in my life. What a relief it was to have Larry help me do that!

I wanted my life clean of anything that might give authority to the devil to claim my life back. I wanted to serve God, and Him alone.

....

I was running. I had just finished guiding a Catholic tour group and I was afraid of being late for this grand event. I wanted to participate in all of it! I wasn't sure my dress was all right though, as I didn't have many clothes left. But I knew that my God loved me anyway.

The big, tall "Building of the Nations" appeared in front of me. This building, called Binianey Haumah in Hebrew, was hosting the annual celebration of the Feast of Tabernacles (called Sukkot in Hebrew), as commanded in the Bible.

The building was packed with Christians from all over the world in beautiful garments. Some were dancers, some musicians or artists. They were all vibrant and happy and full of love. My heart said, this is the kingdom of God and I belong to this kingdom now. These people are my spiritual family. I am not alone! I have a spiritual family all over the world! How exciting!

The music started and people all over the hall lifted holy hands in praise and worship to Jesus and began worshipping him in unknown tongues. Then the distinct presence of the Holy Spirit of the God of Israel filled the hall! A subtle gush of wind refreshed us and an atmosphere of sweetness permeated the place as the love of God permeated our hearts.

Yeshua, Jesus, how beautiful you are, and how real!

******

"O Father!" I prayed. "The children are coming to spend the weekend with me, and I need help. I am still so weak and hurt." Even though God's Spirit was healing me, I still needed patience, as healing in most cases is a process. The door bell rang.

"Anne, what are you doing here?" I gasped, surprised. Anne Louek was standing at the door with a big suitcase.

"Well," she said, "you told me that if I ever need a place to stay, I can stay with you."

"Come in!" I told her happily. "I meant what I said, so welcome home!"

I had met Anne during the celebration of the Feast of Tabernacles and liked her instantly. There was something refreshing about her childlike faith in the Lord. She was sweet, and she had a healthy sense of humor.

"I'm delighted to see you!" I said. "I was just praying for the Lord to send me some help this weekend, since my children are coming, and I am still not fully healed. Regard yourself as an answer to my prayers!"

******

My little apartment home became a house of prayer. People were coming and going all the time. We would pray, talk about the Lord, read the Bible, or worship God with guitars and song. It was like going to a church meeting every day.

"Dominiquae," Batya suggested one day, "don't you think that you should go back to your original name, Ronit?" Batya was the wife of the spiritual leader of the congregation of Messianic believers that I attended. "How do you know that this name was given to you by God?"

"Well," I said, "it means 'the lady of the Lord,' or 'God's property.' And besides, I know beyond a shadow of a doubt that God gave me this name while I was still in the midst of my occultic experience. It was God's way of telling the devil he had to let go of me, since I was 'God's property.'"

She still doubted, but I knew in my heart that this was true. I still remembered the old pastor of the Catholic group that I was guiding when God had spoken to me at the Sea of Galilee. He was a very quiet man and had been fasting and praying that day, in deep meditation.

"Here," he had said, handing me a small piece of paper. "This is your name from God, not 'Dominique,' but 'Dominiquae.' The Latin suffix –'ae' means that you are God's property."

God had spoken to him about my name, and I wasn't going to give up this new name that proclaimed, every time it was spoken or written, that I was God's property! On the practical level, I had already changed all my papers to this name. No, I was happy with my new name!

******

Nora was as white as if she had seen a ghost. "Dominiquae, I must speak to you before you start the tour today!"

"Sure," I told her. "Let's stand here on the side of the hotel."

Nora was one of the sweet ladies in this American-Cuban group of tourists that I was guiding. They were all Christians, filled with the Holy Spirit. I was really enjoying myself!

Nora proceeded with a serious look on her face. "He woke me up at four in the morning, and I saw Jesus! He touched my feet to wake me and then he started speaking to me. He said, 'Go to Dominiquae, Nora, before she starts the tour today. Tell her not to be afraid. Tell her that I have posted angels around her, like the lights of Jerusalem. And I have given her a gift of grace to attract people, like bees are attracted to honey. She will go to places and tell people that she has come from a land where the great King was born. Tell her that because she has been faithful in the little things, I will entrust her with much.'"

I was touched to the core of my being! Jesus had appeared to Nora for the sole purpose of giving me a prophetic word concerning my future in him! I knew that this didn't happen every day.

Nora was still shaken. It was an amazing experience to her.

I hugged her. "Thank you for being obedient and for coming to me. God bless you!" Yeshua, my heart said, I love you, and I will serve you and go wherever you'll take me!

Little did I know that this promise was recorded in heaven, to be required of me soon, — very soon!

Chapter 18

Thy Kingdom Come, Thy Will Be Done

"Flight 717 to London will take off in twenty minutes."

I was exhilarated! I had never traveled with Jesus before. It is so real to walk with Jesus that I didn't feel alone at all. I had just spent invaluable minutes in the airport synagogue, praying before the flight. "O God," I prayed, "open the eyes of my people to see that you are the Messiah of Israel!"

This would be one of the many times that I would cry out before God for the salvation of my people, Israel. I knew that the prophetic time was ripe for the Jewish people to discover who the Messiah really is. But it wasn't only for the Jewish people that I would be crying later on, but for the whole world to recognize Jesus, the Son of God, the Messiah of Israel as the only way, the only salvation for this dark and demon-possessed world.

"Dominiquae," Larry had said before he left for England, "why don't you come spend a month in my parents' home, as my guest? You can attend our church and become stronger, as we help you to walk the Christian road."

I wasn't very sure. "If the Lord permits me, I'll come. I don't want to do anything that God doesn't want me doing."

"That's all right. Give me an answer by mail, as I by faith start preparing for your coming."

Here I was — three months later, about to board a plane for England!

****

Larry and I had fallen in love. It seemed inevitable, and we believed that it was God's will for us to be married. We were feverishly preparing for the wedding.

Some of the people around us were not happy about it, but others were elated. "Isn't it just like the Lord to have a Messianic Jew and a Christian Gentile get married?" these people said. "Your wedding will really symbolize the unity between Jews and Gentiles in Christ. "People were talking, and we were going in high gear."

But Larry's best friend advised, "Brother, if this is from God, why don't you wait a few months?"

We were sitting one day at the home of an elderly couple, friends of Larry's. Mr. S. said emphatically, "I have never believed that a divorced woman should marry again. It cannot succeed!"

His wife nodded in agreement. "We don't approve of your plans."

These people were not mincing any words, and I was feeling very uncomfortable. Hadn't I become a new person when I accepted my Messiah's atonement for sin? Didn't the Bible say that "the old is gone, the new has come"? Will I have to carry the failures of the past with me?

On the other hand, a little voice was saying inside, "Is Larry really my God-appointed husband?" Oh, what a headache all this was!

"Yes!"

"God, my God! My dear Lord, what is happening? Please, Lord, talk to me! Is this wedding really from You?" There was only silence from the other end of the line to heaven.

I often talked to the Lord, and heard a sweet voice whispering into my heart. But this time I couldn't hear anything clearly. My soul was in tremendous anguish. Peace was far away from me. Suddenly, with a burst of clarity, I fell on my knees and prayed, "Lord, I let go of this wedding! I put it on the altar! If this is not from you, cancel it, Lord, and help me to regain my peace!"

This was five days before my wedding date. I had arrived in England a month earlier, and without knowing it, had become involved in this unnecessary relationship. My soul was still too fresh concerning my past, and I was a victim of my own wounded emotional state.

After praying that prayer, the peace came again, but with a mixture of sadness and deep grief. For what had I come to England, after all?

******

"You must stop being Jewish." The words echoed in my heart and pierced me with desperation. "You are a witch!" Ringing, ringing in my ears, cruel words, wounding, poisoned arrows. "The wedding is off!" Larry had said, with a cold, detached voice. His eyes looked wild.

His friend and "big brother," George, had looked at me with eyes full of hate. "You have accepted Christ, and you must stop being Jewish now. Larry has been bewitched by you."

I was tossing and turning on my bed. I couldn't sleep. I only prayed, "O God! Let me die!" The turmoil in my soul would not let go. I was still in Larry's home, in the guest bedroom. At least I hadn't been thrown out into the street last night. Nothing would comfort me.

"All right, Lord," I said, "if you don't help me to kill myself, at least help me to reach my Bible, so that you can speak to me."

The strength of God's Holy Spirit came immediately into my body. As that happened, I grabbed my Bible and it flung open to Psalm 27.

The Lord is my light and my salvation: whom shall I fear? The Lord is the strength of my life; of whom shall I be afraid?

Deliver me not over unto the will of mine enemies: for false witnesses are risen up against me, and such as breathe out cruelty.

I had fainted, unless I had believed to see the goodness of the Lord in the land of the living.

Wait on the Lord: be of good courage, and he shall strengthen thine heart: wait, I say, on the lord!

I understood that God was telling me to wait and to do nothing in haste. He surely had a solution for me and it would be revealed soon. I took a deep breath and prepared myself to wait for some miracle to happen.

******

There were three light knocks on my door.

"Come in," I called. I was white as a sheet. The shock because of the way this wedding was put off had still not left me. I was just obeying God, who had spoken to me through Psalm 27, to wait on the Lord. I was waiting for a miracle. I needed somebody to help me get to the nearest travel agency to purchase a ticket for the next flight to Israel.

Sixteen year old Michelle came into the room. She took one look at me, and knew that I was more dead than alive! She opened her arms and hugged me! I sensed the warmth and love of my Lord emanating from her and broke into tears for the first time since the abrupt news was announced the previous night. The love of Yeshua through Michelle caused me to want to hang onto life, after all.

******

"Good morning," said Jenny in a cheerful voice. "Here, have some home-made cookies and mint tea. I want you to rest. Stay in bed for as long as the Lord wants you to. You need to spend time alone with God. Feel at home, please!"

"Thank you, Jenny," I said in a weak voice. "But I don't know what to do. I bought this ticket to Israel in a rush, so that I could leave this place as soon as possible. Now I don't know if I will be able to be on that flight, as I feel weak."

"Dominiquae, our Father in heaven is taking care of you. Don't worry about the ticket! He can always provide another one for you — when the time comes. Meanwhile, just rest, and strengthen yourself in the Lord." With these words she left the room.

Dear Jenny had been used by the Lord to literally save my life. Her husband, Geoffrey, and she were elders at the Banham Right-Hand Christian Community Church. This was a beautiful group of non-denominational Christians who met in a barn for church services. This had been the first church I attended after arriving in England, in the county of Norfolk where Larry lived.

News travels fast in small places, and the news about Larry cancelling the wedding had reached Jenny the following morning. She had immediately called Larry's home and had offered me her home as a refuge, for as long as I needed it. In spite of my foolishness, God was there to help me, and pick me up again!

Jenny and Geoffrey Darrah were, and still are, lovers of Israel and the Jewish people. Through the next four months they would become a spiritual father and mother to me. Thanks to their love, hospitality, and their true Christian example before me, I learned principles and fundamentals of the faith that would guide me for years to come, as I walked on the narrow way of eternal life.

******

I had spent nearly two weeks in bed. My heart was slowly recovering. I never checked it medically, but due to the trauma my heart had suffered I had continuous pain in my chest. I knew that a little more stress might cause it irreparable damage.

During those two weeks I had regained a relationship with God's Holy Spirit on a totally new level. This period of brokenness caused me to surrender my will totally to the Lord. Never again would I be led by emotions or by other voices. Something had happened in me. A depth of understanding of the ways of God and His voice had come. A rapid process of growth in the things of God had begun. I indeed came to England to be prepared for marriage. But it wasn't to Larry!

I learned to have an intimacy with God that would accompany me for all the years to come. This time of suffering and humiliation was turned by the Lord for "the good of those who love him," and I would never be the same again. My will became totally surrendered to his will, to this day. I will do whatever He wants me to do, and I will go wherever He sends me.

******

"Jenny," I said joyfully and full of faith and health, "the Lord has supplied a job for me as a nanny for three little girls. The mother has gone through a terrible time in which she almost lost her life after the cesarean operation of her last baby. She said that I would be like a Christmas present to her."

Jenny looked satisfied with the information. "Yes," she said. "It seems that the Lord has opened this door to you."

A few days later I kissed Jenny and Geoffrey goodbye as I went off to care for these three little girls. I was not aware that God was preparing a real surprise for me. This job was not only going to be a blessing to a desperate mother and a needy family, but it was to be a tool in God's hands to heal me for the loss of my own children. I had a heart full of unused motherly love to give to Rossana, Alexia, and baby Sabrina!

Chris and Coral McEwen were a beautiful, well educated English couple. Chris being a Catholic, and Coral an Anglican, did not oppose my teaching the girls about the Lord Jesus, Yeshua. They knew that I was non-denominational, spoke in tongues and raised my hands in church shouting hallelujahs pretty often!

I would not deny the reality of the infilling of the Holy Spirit and his power. God's reality and power were the only things that could have healed and delivered me. Besides, it is His will for every Christian to be filled with His Spirit. Coral had said upon my arrival, "I am giving you permission and freedom to discipline and take care of my girls, as if I were the one doing it." This was a privilege, entrusting me with their most precious possession — their daughters!

After the five weeks of this temporary job had ended, none of us were sorry for this mutual trust. I had fallen in love with "my" girls, and had treated them as if I had given birth to them myself. The whole family was as friendly to me as if I'd been a natural part of the family. I will never forget the McEwens. God bless them!

Chapter 19

Life Is Good

I had just come home to Jenny and Geoffrey's, where I stayed between jobs. I was working and saving some money to start over when I returned to Israel. Tomorrow I would be traveling to Scotland, for I had obtained a job to work for a month at a Christian ski resort.

The Lord is always more generous than we expect. He had provided this job for me at the Glencoe Outdoor Center. They would pay my train fare, provide my food and lodging, and pay a weekly salary in addition. Besides that, I was promised free ski lessons!

As I was packing for Scotland that day, in late February, I decided to listen to a tape by a well-known lover of Israel, the Bible teacher Derek Prince.

As the tape began, I sat quietly on the carpet in the cozy den, listening intently to his words. The tape was his message at a conference in Israel during the Feast of Pentecost. Many Christians and Messianic Jews had come together for this meeting. The atmosphere was charged with expectancy.

After talking for a few minutes about the Lord coming very soon, Derek told of the need for people to volunteer themselves to God. The Lord wanted volunteers to be sent out into the world to tell people everywhere of the good news of the kingdom of God and salvation.

"Would you be willing to work for God, and to be sent out?" he asked.

My heart began beating rapidly. I felt I had to stand up in front of this tape, and in front of God, and commit myself to become an ambassador for God. "But God," I said, "how can I go? I have children in Israel. How can I leave them?"

The Holy Spirit was grieved. Hadn't I surrendered my will to him? Isn't God well able to take care of all details? Didn't I owe my every breath to the Lord? He had made me sane and healthy. Wasn't the first commandment to love the Lord my God with all my heart, and mind, and strength, about everything?

"God," I cried out, "please let me rewind the tape and answer the call. Forgive me for hesitating!"

I rewound the tape. When the call came from Derek Prince to "stand up and come forth, commit yourself to be sent out," I stood up in the little den, all alone, in front of the tape player.

"God," I said, "I am willing to become your ambassador, to preach your gospel and to serve you, whatever it takes!"

The joy of the Holy Spirit flooded me and I felt as light as if I could fly! I spun around and screamed, "Hallelujah! I am a servant of God, and there is a purpose for my life after all!!!"

I did not know when I could expect God to "collect" on this commitment, and send me out.

******

I was huffing and puffing, climbing a very high mountain peak. It was beautiful, full of snow. The wind was coming strongly against my body, bitingly cold against my face. But I was pressing on, climbing up with a backpack on my back.

"Yes!"

The other people didn't seem to be having problems like I was having, climbing up the mountain. They had been doing it for months, and some for years. And I intended to do it too. I would get up there! It was a challenge for me.

Someone looked around and said, "Dominiquae, are you all right?" I just nodded my head and kept going up. It was so cold!

This was Scotland, in March, 1989. Scotland was bitterly cold, but I had decided that if God had sent me here to work with the Christian ski center, I could do it. I didn't take into consideration that I had gone through tremendously devastating experiences within the last year, and that my physical body still needed to be built up after all those traumas. I knew just one thing: "I am going to make it!"

I was laughing inside. Part of me was laughing, and part of me was crying, because I was wearing five layers of clothes, five layers of socks, and shoes three times larger than my own size. I felt like a huge bear trying to lumber up the mountain.

Finally I arrived, entering the little ski hut where I would be taught how to rent the skis, fix them, and match them to the people when they came to rent them. I took the backpack off my shoulders, and put it down with a sigh of relief.

The manager noticed how pale I was and asked, "How are you doing?"

"Brother, I'm all right, but I'm frozen down to my toes!"

"Oh," he said, "here. Put this little packet inside your shoes, you'll soon feel the warmth spreading and you'll be able to warm up."

"Praise God! Give it to me."

I put it inside my shoes and managed to function for a few more hours, but I was getting more and more despondent and depressed. I was trying to make it, but the cold was reaching all the way to my bones! I didn't realize that an Israeli girl who's used to summer and the heat and warmth of the Tel Aviv area, could not easily adjust to a place like this, on the Argyle coast of Scotland.

"Dominiquae, are you all right?" It was the end of the day. The lady who owned the ski center was looking at me with concern.

"Well, ummm, since you asked," I mumbled, "I'll tell you the truth. I am really suffering from the cold."

She could see that I looked very despondent. "Yes," she said, "you're suffering from hypothermia. Your body heat is too low for you to keep on going like this. What do you suggest we do?"

I looked at her for a moment, and then said, "We can pray and ask God to keep helping me."

"You know," she replied thoughtfully, "we've been trying to get a cook up here for the last few months. We finally found one, but she's only able to come a month from now. That means that I'll have to do all the cooking for this month, and my husband and I have enough work to do already. Do you think you could do the cooking, instead of coming up here to work in the ski hut? That way you wouldn't have to come up the mountain at all. You could stay in the hotel taking care of the kitchen. That would give you a lot of free time too. We'll even pay you extra for that."

It was as if an angel were talking! I looked at her in astonishment, smiled, and radiance came back into my soul! "Are you kidding?" I asked. "I'll take the job right away!"

Hallelujah, my heart cried. God, thank you for your help! You knew I couldn't take the cold any more!

I went down the mountain that day with a happy heart, to become the cook for this outdoor ski resort. Of course, I did not take into consideration the fact that I had never cooked in a recreation center before, that I had never cooked English food — or Scottish food either, for that matter. Nor did I take into consideration that I would not be cooking for five people, but for 50 or 60 people, depending on how many came from time to time.

But I did not worry over these petty matters. I had a big God living in me and I knew one thing: Yeshua, my Lord, is the best cook and nutritionist one could ever find in the whole world. If I relied on him and his knowledge, and on his Holy Spirit that he had put in me, I would be able to cook.

******

I had been in Scotland for nearly a month. It had been a most productive month, enjoying the gorgeous mountain peaks in the background. On some sunny days the snow melted down to the village of Glencoe, where the recreation center was. It was beautiful, with greenery all around. The flowers were beginning to bloom and the birds were returning. In spite of the cold, the birds were singing.

And there were some streams flowing from the waterfalls. I would take the bicycle and go around enjoying nature and the Creator of nature. "Praise the Lord!" I was exhilarated. "God, you're so wonderful and good to have led me to a place that is so beautiful. You've given me work as a cook, and I'm learning so much in that. I truly thank you!"

It was at that time that I met Ralph and Mary Kellet Smith. They became my very best friends there. They were Spirit-filled Christians who loved the Lord with all their heart. They were full of zeal for God, and full of laughter. They adopted me as a friend and a part of their family.

Ralph became a big asset to me. Before I came to Scotland I sensed that God was leading me to write down my testimony, telling how he had saved me. I had prayed, "Lord, if you really want me to write my testimony, then you'll need to provide at least a month in which to do it, and then somebody to type it and correct my English."

I could not have known that God had provided a month's refuge in Scotland where I would have much free time. While the others were up on the mountain, I was writing my story down! The Lord had also provided Ralph to help me, editing my testimony and correcting my English mistakes. Ralph and Mary were a blessing to me, and I to them. And God had orchestrated the whole thing!

Chapter 20

The Still, Small Voice

I was invited to a covered-dish party that was to be at Ralph and Mary's home one evening. It was called a "pot-blessing," rather than a "potluck" party. Mary invited everyone to bring something. But she said to me, "Because you don't have your own home, you just come. Don't worry about bringing any food."

Even though I was the cook at the resort hotel, it wasn't my own food, but my heart wanted to give. I prayed, "Lord, I really want to bring something. What can I do?"

After lunch one day there was big amount of rice left over. I knew one thing. If there were any leftovers, unless I did something with them, they would be thrown out. I didn't like people throwing out food so easily.

The pot-blessing was planned for that evening. I prayed, "Lord, what can I do?"

The Holy Spirit impressed on me to look in the refrigerator. There was this big amount of rice that was left, and he said, "Just take the rice with you."

It was just plain rice, and I had a little pride in my heart. "Oh God," I said, "Am I to bring only this? First of all, it's not my rice, Lord." This was not really true — for it would just be thrown out. But I felt it wasn't mine. And I argued,

"Only plain rice, Lord? When I'm the cook, I should bring something more elaborate."

I was wrestling with the voice of the Lord. When God speaks to his people, it is often in a very little, gentle voice in one's heart, through the Holy Spirit. I did not obey his voice, and I learned a big lesson!

I walked up the beautiful drive to Ralph and Mary's house. By the time I arrived a big party was already going on. The people were all there, and had brought some wonderful dishes. They were sitting down, talking to each other. I was received with warmth and affection and given a place to sit. I could see a gorgeous view of the lake from where I was sitting. It was a blessed time.

Suddenly Mary said, "I wonder what's happened to Mrs. So-and-So (I don't recall the name)? She was supposed to bring the rice for the curry. We have curry here, but the rice hasn't come, and it's time to start eating. What do we do?"

I looked toward Mary. My heart said, "See? I told you to bring the rice." But I disregarded that voice again.

Time passed, and Mary became more and more concerned. Finally she got up and said, "Well, we'll just have to start eating the curry without the rice, because she still hasn't come, and everything else is ready."

I felt such deep conviction! Oh, my God, I thought, you told me to bring rice, even though I wasn't the one appointed to bring it. You knew, in your wisdom, that the lady who was to bring it would be late, and unless I brought the rice, there would be none for the curry.

Of course, to the simple mind, this might sound very foolish. Why would a big God care if we have rice for the curry, or not? But he does. He cares for even those little details. He also cares whether or not his people obey his still, small voice when he speaks to our hearts, even in these seemingly foolish things of the world.

So I rose up, fully repenting. "Mary," I said, in front of everyone, "I want to confess a sin."

"Yes? What happened?"

In front of them all I said, "Before I left the kitchen today at the ski center, the Lord told me to bring the rice that was left over, but because of my embarrassment and pride, I thought, 'No, this is only plain rice, and it's not even mine.' I refused to bring it."

There was a holy hush in the room. Mary looked at me, saying, "Dominiquae, you should know better than not to obey the voice of the Lord. We could have had rice with this curry, don't you know?"

Blushing, I told her, "Mary, please forgive me. I have learned a big lesson today."

They all blessed the food and began eating, even the curry without the rice. I felt so embarrassed throughout the evening that I was the one that caused that!

Later, the woman who was to bring the rice arrived, after the curry was all gone. "I'm so sorry," she explained, "but I was unavoidably delayed so that I couldn't be here in time. I knew you needed the rice, but what could I do?"

"It's not your fault," I told her. "God had already covered for you, but I disobeyed him."

I had learned my lesson. From that day on, I have known that whenever God's Holy Spirit speaks to my heart, I am going to do whatever he says. And if I don't, I will miss his best for me, and for other people.

******

It was time to leave England and return to Israel. I said goodbye to my friends at the ski center and to all the other friends I had made. The ones I really grieved over leaving were Ralph and Mary Kellet Smith, for they had become family to me. But we hugged and said our goodbyes, knowing

"Yes!"

that we would see each other again. We would be in touch, if not on this earth, then in the heavenly realms.

I boarded the train taking me back into England again, very excited. It was April, 1989. My ticket was already purchased for the return to Israel. As the train rumbled along, my memories went back to the time when I had lost the ticket, when I had been so shocked because Larry had called off the wedding.

When Jenny and Geoffrey had taken me into their home Jenny had said, "It might be that it's not time for you to leave. It might be that the Lord wants you here for a time. Don't worry about your ticket. God can always provide another one." She looked up with her eyes to heaven and said in the most matter-of-fact tone, "Father in heaven, thank you for another ticket." That was just a simple prayer!

After the Sunday morning service a few days later, a woman came over to me. "Dominiquae," she said, "I have your ticket to go back to Israel. Whenever you need it, I will pay for it."

So God had answered Jenny's prayer right away with no problem, and in a couple of days I had another ticket. The ticket was paid for, and I was to return to Israel on April 5th.

It was exactly a year before, on April 7th that I had left my family and my children. A whole year had gone by! So many things had happened.

The most important thing was the salvation of my soul, by accepting Yeshua, Jesus the Messiah, the Son of God. During this past year he had redeemed my life, had been rebuilding it, and was making a woman out of me again. God had done so much for me! Just a year after that catastrophic experience, I was a different person, leaving Scotland to return to England and back home to Israel.

This time I was returning not as a shattered, broken, crushed individual with no hope for life, but as a woman of

God, full of faith, full of strength, full of the word of God in my heart, and full of hope for a bright, new future. Yes, indeed God had done so much for me! He had healed me. He had healed my soul and my body. He had saved me from many things.

There was still a road for me to walk, still many things to be set free from, but I was a different person now. I had confidence in my God, who had shown me His faithfulness and had led me lovingly in every way since I had accepted Him.

On the train all these experiences passed through my mind, bringing a mental balance to all that had happened before. I decided, right on that train, that this trip was indeed taking me back to Israel, but my life was never going to be the same again! My life would count for God, and I would do whatever His will might be for my life.

The train pulled into the station. As I left the train, I took my suitcases, expecting Jenny and Geoffrey to be there waiting for me. It was a great joy to see them again. I recounted all the things that had happened to me. "You cannot even imagine," I told them, "all that God has done for me in Scotland. He has healed so much!"

Chapter 21

Dance For Joy

There were only three days before it would be time to leave, but I had so much to tell Jenny and Geoffrey that I talked almost non-stop. I wanted to tell them all about the wonderful things God had done in Scotland, healing me, and using me.

"Jenny, I have to thank you," I told her, "because I watched you cooking before I left. That gave me a real desire to bless people through cooking and baking. I've always loved doing it, but watching you I learned so many things that helped me when I became the cook at the ski center."

Jenny smiled. "I'm happy about that. I've always enjoyed cooking, because it blesses people."

"Yes," I said, "but I had to cook for 50 or 60 people, and many things happened during my time in the kitchen. One Friday I had to cook sweet and sour pork. It didn't bother me to fix it, since I knew that God would bless it, even though pork is not kosher according to Jewish law.

"But while I was cooking the sweet and sour pork, I suddenly became very nauseous. I wanted to taste it to see if it was well done, but I couldn't. I felt violently ill, just looking at it! I couldn't understand it. Then I felt the Holy Spirit was forbidding me to eat pork again. I understood that he was telling me that even though I was saved, I was to remain Jewish. I was not exempted from keeping His laws as he wrote them in the Old Testament. Those laws are for my own good."

Jenny listened, smiling. She understood.

"Therefore, from then on," I went on, "I understood that I am not to eat non-kosher food. God is still keeping me Jewish both as a witness to my own people, and to keep His covenant. I understood that even though the Lord can bless whatever we eat, there are still laws we have to abide by. But He writes those laws in our hearts. I'm not enslaved to those laws, but the Holy Spirit had written that law in my heart: 'Pork is a no.'

"Of course," I went on, "as a nutritionist I know that pork is very unhealthy for people because it is so high in fat content, and because it is an animal that eats garbage. So I had no problem in not eating the pork I was cooking. It was really a peculiar experience to cook for so many people, and not even be able to taste it."

And on and on I went, until finally Jenny said, "Do you have many things to pack for Israel? You only have three days."

"Actually," I said, "the truth is that I have far more things than I'm allowed to take. I am only allowed 20 pounds in the airplane, as it's a small carrier. So unless I have a miracle from God, I'll have to pay a tremendous amount for the extra weight. It may not be worth it."

"We'll pray about it," Jenny said, "and the Lord will open a way. He will do what He always does. He will do a miracle for you."

The next morning I rose early, but before packing, I began praying and communing with the Holy Spirit. "Lord," I said, "you know that I have too much weight. You know, Lord, that there's no way that I will be able to get it all on the airplane unless you do a miracle for me. Either you will blind their eyes, or you will cause the weight of my luggage to be low, or you will show me what to leave behind."

As I was packing, I realized I didn't have many things I could leave behind, for most of them were basic things. Some of them were books that were very important to me. I would need these back in Israel, to help me and help other people. I also had some cooking utensils I had bought in England, as I had decided to become a cook for the whole body of Christ.

I had a desire to start a little business as a caterer, or to bake for special functions. The Lord had given me a wonderful anointing to be able to cook and bake. In my heart I felt this was a calling from God, to bless people in this way.

I was not even faintly aware that God was preparing me for a mightier calling than I had ever dreamed about. I would indeed be "cooking and baking" for many, by preparing messages from the throne of God and write them for people, and to preach to them. But at that point all I understood was that God had anointed me to minister to people in cooking and baking. So I had bought a lot of little pans, muffin tins and such things that I might not be able to find in Israel, to take back with me. I was relying on the grace of God as I was packing, knowing that most of those things I really had to take with me.

That evening we continued our conversation, sitting at the table. Jenny and Geoffrey were as excited as I was, that my time in England had come to an end, and that they were looking at a real miracle sitting in front of them. That girl they had brought into their home, that broken-hearted, "good-for-nothing" woman who had come to them four months earlier, had really blossomed. Now she was a bloom fragrant with the Holy Spirit, full of fire for God, full of strength to go back to her home, to Israel. She was no longer a lame or crippled person, but was one who had been made whole.

"The Lord used me in Scotland for something else very special."

"What was that, Dominiquae?" Jenny asked.

"Well," I explained, "I met a Christian there who had been praying for years for God to send someone to teach them Israeli dancing. She was a schoolteacher. The children in her class had been praying that God would send someone to them to teach them Israeli dancing. But Israel was very far away from where they lived, on the Argyle coast of Scotland."

"I laughed and told her, 'I am the one! I have my Israeli dancing tapes with me. I can teach you all how to dance Israeli folk dancing, and biblical dancing too.'

"You cannot imagine, Jenny, how this woman jumped up and down, saying 'God is so good! He's answered our prayers! All the way from Israel, from Jerusalem, to this little village in Scotland, He's sent a woman to teach us Israeli dancing!'"

"This is indeed the Lord," Jenny laughed. "God does these things! He can send a person from one place to another, anywhere in the world, just because someone prayed!"

"Yes," I said. "I went to the school and taught the children to dance, folk dancing, and Israeli dancing. The people were so blessed!"

As we were talking, we recalled the Israeli evening that she and Geoffrey had organized before I left for Scotland. Since they were the leaders in their fellowship, they had sponsored this for the whole church, to be held in the town hall.

Everyone had come, even people from outside the town. The hall had never been so packed as when this Israeli evening was organized. I had taught them about Israel and its culture, and I had also taught them to dance Israeli dancing. We laughed and rejoiced as we remembered that evening.

"Yes!"

Geoffrey said, "The church was pretty perky after that Israeli evening. Everyone was up on their toes, dancing in the church. There was a spirit of joy!"

At that time I still had no idea how God would use these biblical dances in many ways to touch Christians in churches in many places so that the spirit of joy would break through, flooding the people of God with special joy. He was going to use those simple things that I knew, like the Israeli dancing that I grew up with, to bless others.

I thought that cooking, and baking, and dancing were not important. They were just simple things that I knew how to do. But already, God Almighty had been taking things that were simple, that seemed to be foolish, and was beginning to use them mightily in His kingdom.

Jenny, Geoffrey and I joined hands in prayer, committing all these things to the Lord. We prayed for the reconciliation of the church in Israel. We prayed for many things, knowing that in just a couple more days we would have to say goodbye.

"Flight 217 to Tel Aviv will be leaving in 20 minutes. All the passengers are required to board the plane. I repeat, all passengers must board at this time."

Jenny and Geoffrey were with me, and they would not leave until I had gone through the line with my luggage. I knew one thing: I had 40 pounds instead of 20, and I needed a miracle! Paying for the 20 additional pounds would have made me penniless.

"O God, please help!" I prayed ceaselessly. "O Lord, please God, please send help from the heavens to me. "O Lord, help me! Help me!"

As I was putting my luggage on the scales, I left the heaviest one to carry on the plane, the one with all the books. It would really be an ordeal, as it would be heavy for me to carry that bag, but, if it meant paying for 15 or 20 pounds less, I would do it. I had carefully packed this carry-on full of books ahead of time. It was tremendously heavy.

I was holding this bag when the steward who was doing the weighing said, "Please put that bag on the scales also to weigh. We want to take it for you. Don't take it on the plane with you, it would be very uncomfortable."

"No," I started to say, "it's better that I —."

"No," he interrupted, "we are not going to allow this bag to go with you."

So I put it on the scales, and it went. It all went!

The steward looked at me and said, "That will be all." He gave me the tags; I put them on all the suitcases. Then he took all my suitcases and turned to the next person.

I was absolutely amazed! I turned to Jenny and Geoffrey, who were laughing. "Do you realize," I exclaimed to them, "that I just received 20 pounds overweight, for free?"

"Didn't we tell you," they replied, "that if we just prayed, God would do a miracle for you?"

I rejoiced, and laughed, and hugged them, and cried. They laid their hands on me and blessed me. Tears were shed as we parted from each other, and they sent me on my way back to Israel, fully equipped to meet my destiny.

Chapter 22

A Mother's Heart

During the night before I left England I had asked the Lord, "I haven't seen my children in four and a half months. How can I relate to them? They are so small and they've again missed their mother for so long."

After praying I had fallen asleep, and had a dream. In that dream I was sleeping in the same room where my children had their bedroom when Danny and I were still married. I saw Yuval's crib where he slept in when he was a little baby. I saw the special junior bed that Adi slept in. It was like a hide-a-bed that opened up and had enough space for even two people to sleep in. All night in my dream, I slept next to Adi on the hide-a-bed, while Yuval slept in his crib close by. Throughout the whole dream, I slept in their room.

In the morning when I woke up, I knew I had slept all night in the room with my children when they were smaller. "Lord," I said, my heart throbbing, "what does this mean? How can I sleep in the same room? We don't have this house any more. Danny and I are divorced!"

The Lord said to me, "You have slept the whole night in your children's bedroom. Now go back and behave as if you've never left them. Don't make a big fuss. Don't be dramatic. Just say, 'Hello,' and begin a normal life with them

"Yes!"

as if you'd never left, as if you'd been sleeping with them in their room all these past months." That was the advice I was given, directly from the Spirit of God.

As I was arriving in Israel and when the plane had just landed in the Tel Aviv airport, I knew one thing — I was not to make a big fuss! I was just to hug them, love them, immediately show them their wonderful presents I'd bought for them, and be my normal self without apologies. Adi would be turning six in a month, and Yuval would soon be two and a half years old.

I started walking through customs. I passed customs, and as I was walking out I caught a glimpse of the people who were waiting for the passengers of this plane. I could see my mother and little Adi, eagerly waiting for her mommy.

I ran to Adi and hugged her! She shyly looked at me, without a word.

Don't be dramatic, I said to myself. The Lord said not to be dramatic. So I just said, "Hello, Adi! Hello! I love you! I'm so happy to see you! I brought you the most wonderful presents!"

Adi was very excited when she heard the word "presents." I had a few in my handbag. "Here, you take this one, and this one, and we'll open them. There are many more to come. The rest are in my luggage."

Of course all the presents mommy had brought distracted her attention while I hugged my mother and said, "Hello, mommy. How are you doing?"

"Well, it could be better," she said. "Daddy's not doing very well. I want you to be prepared for something you haven't seen before."

My dad had been ill with cancer for the last year. Even before I left my dad had been in a very bad state. I had not seen him for the last four and a half months, being in England. It seemed now his situation was deteriorating.

"Yes!"

"It's very bad," mom told me. "We still believe there might be hope, but it's very bad."

I was sad for my daddy. The Lord had done a tremendous healing in my heart concerning my family. I had no resentment against them, and no unforgiveness at all. I only had love for them. I wanted them all healthy and whole and godly.

I hugged my mom again saying, "God is good. God is able to do a miracle for us."

"Yes, I believe that," she answered. My mother believes in God in her own way, but it's not the godly way, not the way of the Bible. It is the way that she has made up in her own mind, according to the New Age philosophies.

But I didn't say this. I just hugged her again, loving her and said, "Mommy, God is able. We can pray."

We went to the car and drove all the way back to Raanana, which is on the northern side of Tel Aviv where my parents lived. Adi was so excited. I kept hugging her, happy to be with my daughter and longing to see my son.

As soon as we arrived at home, and I had brought all my things inside, I said, "Come on, let's go see Yuval!" So we took off again to my in-laws home, where he was.

I'll never forget that reunion with my son. Yuval was two and a half years old and had only seen his mother on and off for a whole year. He had been a little baby, just a little over a year old, when he had lost his mommy. I had not been there from then on, only on and off,

I arrived and opened the gate to the garden. Their home is in one of the most beautiful suburbs in the whole of Israel. As I was entering the gate Yuval came out of the house and stared at me, not saying anything, and I feasted my eyes on him, unable to say a word for a moment. He was such a sturdy, handsome little boy! "Shalom, Yuval!" I said.

Yuval ran into my arms as if he'd recognize me among a million people! He hugged me and hugged me.

"Yuval, I'm your mommy!"

"Mommy," he cried, hugging me as tightly as he could. "Shalom, mommy!" I remembered my dream the night before when God had told me, "It's going to be as if you'd never left them at all." I kept hugging Yuval and couldn't let go of him. Adi threw her arms around us, and we three were just hugging and loving each other, so happy to be together again!

"Yuval, I've brought you some presents." And we all began opening the presents.

It was a special time for me to have my children back again, and to have their love as if I'd never left them at all. In my heart I was praising and thanking God that in spite of all the adverse circumstances, and the tragedy around us, he'd kept my children's love for me intact, and my love for them too. I knew that was a miracle.

What I didn't know was that I would have to deal with the very bitter father of these children. I didn't know how bitter Danny had become these last few months. He didn't accept any letters of reconciliation I had been sending him. He had rejected them. He would not accept my apology and my plea for forgiveness, but had grown increasingly bitter.

I greeted him and gave him my hand. "How are you?" I asked. I was full of love for him because God had put a tremendous love in my heart for anyone and everyone. In my heart I had no problem with anyone who had ever hurt me, because of the love of the Holy Spirit within.

Chapter 23

The Lord Is My Shepherd

"Daddy, what are you eating?" I asked. He was so thin. He looked like a walking cadaver, a walking skeleton. The skin was shrunken over his skull, his eyes were sunk deep in their sockets, and his abdomen was bloated. The cancer was eating him up.

"Daddy, what have you been eating? Who has been nourishing you?"

He showed me the type of foods he was eating. He had been going to health food consultants, but I hadn't been there to help him.

"Daddy," I told him, "I'm going to feed you some things that will strengthen you, and bring your weight up a little. Come to the kitchen with me."

He could barely walk, but he followed me. I started preparing some yogurt with fruit and honey, and things that would really encourage him. My dad always liked good food, especially things that were a little sweeter. So I made things sweet for him, to please him.

I wanted so much to share my faith in Yeshua with him! I tried, but he would not allow me to say the name "Jesus" in the house. He would not allow me to say "Yeshua." He would become very angry. I wanted so much to say that name, but I couldn't.

But I began sharing with him truths from the Bible. "Father, let me read some Psalms to you." He would listen quietly, very quietly, as I read him the psalms of David from the Bible, psalms of hope.

From the time I arrived home from England, I began feeding my father natural foods, good foods, and also with spiritual food from the Bible. I did not know how crucial this time would be for his salvation, or that God had already given me only ten days before my dad would be taken from this world — only ten days! This was the first of the ten days.

During those ten days my father and I bonded with one another as never before in our entire lives. I loved him, and he loved me. There was real, open communication with him for the first time. All through this time of illness, I nurtured and nursed dad as I had never done before.

But it was really tough for him. He suffered tremendous pain and agony. My mom was very despondent. Even though everyone tried to be hopeful about it, they knew that he was terribly ill. God Almighty had brought me home just ten days before his death — but I did not know that.

"Mommy," I asked, "would you come with me to a special meeting on Saturday night?"

"Are you talking about a Messianic meeting?"

"Yes. It's beautiful. They pray for people, and I think you will enjoy it."

Mother was pretty desperate over the situation with my father. Surprisingly, she said, "Okay. I'll come with you."

Off we went to a place where the Messianic meetings were being held. I didn't know many Jewish believers in Israel, but by the grace of God I had managed to find a phone number, and had learned what time the meeting was held.

Yuval had been given under my care for the weekend, as I had as many visiting rights as I wanted, according to the divorce contract. I took his hand and said, "Yuval, let's go praise God!"

Yuval was delighted to come too. I took along a tambourine and gave it to him to carry. When we arrived at the meeting they were singing and playing musical instruments. I sang and played musical instruments, while little Yuval happily shook the tambourine in time to the music.

My mother saw the atmosphere of God's Holy Spirit, since she is very sensitive to spiritual matters. She knew that there was a presence there that was different and special. I was elated that she was there.

I knew that I would be refreshed. I needed to meet other people who believed like I did. The situation with my family was really tough. My dad was on the verge of death. I needed the prayers of the saints, the fellowship of other Christians and Messianic Jews.

During the meeting the leader of the group stood up and announced, "There's a new congregation being started in the Sharon Valley area." He described the location, and it was only about ten minutes from my mom's house, where I was staying!

"This little congregation has just been birthed," he explained. "It had been a home group, but we are now releasing it to become the Congregation of the Fountain "Hamaayan." Its name is taken from Isaiah 12: 'With joy will you draw water from the fountains of salvation.'"

I was overjoyed! I remembered that when I was flying back to Israel, the Lord had given me Isaiah 12. I had said, "Isaiah 12? Why Isaiah 12? What is God saying to me?"

I had read it, but had had absolutely no idea what the Lord was trying to tell me. Now, sitting in this congregational meeting, hearing Isaiah 12 read, and with the name of this new congregation which was only ten minutes away from where I was living, I knew! The Lord had given me Isaiah 12 to show me where I was to fellowship with other believers, and make it my spiritual home.

I rose up and went to the leader of the new congregation. "My name is Dominiquae," I told him. "The Lord gave me Isaiah 12 before I arrived in Israel. Now I know that God was saying I am to become a member of that new congregation."

All the members of this new congregation were asked to come onto the stage, to have hands laid on them and be blessed. And — though they had not known me from Adam until a few minutes before, they asked me to come on stage with them! They laid hands on me, so that I was publicly welcomed into the body of Christ in Israel.

I hadn't known anyone, and was pretty lonely, but God had made sure I would have a spiritual home in Israel right from the beginning! Isn't God good? He has been so faithful in my life! Little Yuval was with me, experiencing the atmosphere of the Holy Spirit, his little heart wide open to it all.

Mom enjoyed the whole thing and it made her think. God had begun impregnating her with His Word and with His Spirit.

******

"We are going to be teaching today from Romans, chapter one. Everyone open the Bible, and let's learn together from this letter to the Romans."

I opened my Bible. I was so happy to be in this meeting! It was at the home of Tony and Orna, the leaders of this new congregation in the Sharon Valley area. They had accepted me and welcomed me. Now I had a family that was a true family in the Lord.

"Yes!"

As little as this group was, the essence of the love of God was present to embrace new members, and help them to grow. Tony, a very anointed young leader and his wife, Orna, would be leading this congregation from now on, from glory to glory and from strength to strength.

I enjoyed every word as Tony read from the book of Romans. I loved the word of God! He read and he explained, and we debated what the text was all about. He ended the meeting with a prayer, and then we had a snack and some coffee.

I was sitting next to Tony and said, "Tony, my father is about to die if we don't pray for him. He's in a very bad state, with cancer. My mom has allowed me to invite you all to come and pray in the hospital for him, because they've just taken him to the hospital. He has to have an enormous amount of medication, because of the tremendous pain he's in."

"No problem," Tony said. "We'll come and pray around his bed. Tomorrow morning first thing, we'll meet and pray, believing God for a miracle."

I could hardly wait for the morning to come! We all gathered, because my mother had given us permission to pray around his bed at the hospital. We closed the door behind us, because we did not want anyone in the room who did not have the faith to believe God for my father's healing.

I pleaded with my Father in heaven. "God," I said, "in your word it is written that the fervent, effectual prayer of a righteous person avails much. And Lord, I believe I'm a righteous person in your eyes, because I am saved. I received the blood of Jesus, Father, and Yeshua is my Messiah. I'm asking you to heal my dad, and raise him from his bed."

I prayed and prayed, and everyone prayed and prayed. All of a sudden something happened! The Spirit of God fell on me with the spirit of prophecy. I didn't even know what it was at that point. I just knew one thing. I began talking words from God directly to my father's spirit, even though he was unconscious. I spoke in Spanish, his mother-tongue.

I didn't understand at the time that God's Holy Spirit was talking prophetically directly to his spirit, because his spirit was still in him, and he could still hear, though his mind was unconscious. His spirit was alive, listening to what I was saying.

"Father, you have not allowed me to talk about Yeshua, but you must be saved. Yeshua is waiting for you. Accept him! Embrace him in your heart!"

I said all these things to him in Spanish, because he could only speak in Spanish at the end of his life. Being so ill with cancer, it was like the illness had erased every other language he knew. So in Spanish, as the Spirit of God fell upon me, I spoke to him the most piercing words for salvation.

After I had finished those words, we prayed in tongues together around his bed. A quiet, peaceful silence fell over us all, and we knew we had finished our job. We turned around and left the room.

Then we told my mother about it. I said, "Mommy, we've prayed for daddy, and I believe that a miracle has taken place."

My mother was expectant and hopeful, but she had made a mistake. She had another group of people praying for the soul of my father. The only difference was that these people were not Messianic Jews or Christian believers. They were not even godly people. They believed that there is a new dimension in the heavenlies, and that they were receiving directions from masters in the heavens. These were people of the New Age.

They meditated, practicing the occult. They sent their thoughts in what they called the "light," to people who were ill, and to people in other trying situations. My mom was a part of this occult group. The woman in charge was a channeler. She channeled messages to them from the masters in the heavens, whom I knew to be demon spirits. For there is only one Master in heaven, and his name is Yeshua Messiah.

Yeshua said, "I am the way and the truth and the life. No one comes to the Father but through me."

These were demon spirits sending messages to my mother's group. The Bible says, "Do not believe every spirit, but test them, to see if they are from God." I knew this group did not believe in the God of Israel as written in the Bible. They had a new type of religion with all kinds of theories and practices: yoga, meditation, the occult, white witchcraft.

My mother had these people praying for my father's soul, and she also had my Messianic group praying for my father's soul! I sensed that in the heavens there was a tremendous battle between the forces of good and the forces of evil, between the devil and God. But I knew one thing: God Almighty, my Father which is in heaven, is more powerful than anything. I knew the prayers of the saints would prevail against the prayers of those that were in deception.

Our little prayer group had left the hospital on Sunday full of faith, yet knowing it would be God's will concerning my father that would be done. The next morning I arose at five at my mom's house, for at six I was to be at Tony's for a prayer meeting. Every Monday morning there was a prayer meeting in his home.

I took the bus to Tony's and arrived at their home. Eric, another Jewish believer in that congregation was there, as well as Tony and Orna and I. We were four people, praying.

Tony said, "We are going to lift up your father before the Lord again. I'm going to pray for him."

They prayed, "Let your perfect will be done, God, with Dominiquae's father, and let his soul be saved."

"God," I prayed, "you can raise him from the dead, Father. I believe that you can raise him even if he dies, and let him live." Yet something within me said that although

"Yes!"

God had heard all the prayers, his will would be done, and it might not be exactly what I wanted.

We prayed until about seven in the morning. Tony dismissed us and said, "Goodbye. Thank you for coming and being faithful to the Lord."

"Goodbye Tony," I said. "Thank you for being with me at this time and praying with me."

I left, took the bus back to my mom's, opened the door with the key, and found that all the windows were open! Everything was open, the house was in disarray, and there was nobody there! There was a sensation of urgency.

In my heart I knew that they had gone to the hospital because my father had passed away. I knew by the Holy Spirit that he had passed away from this earth. As this awareness came, I ran to my car and drove to the hospital. I don't know how I even managed to drive, for the tears were streaming down from my eyes. I knew I'd lost my dad.

I'd just begun to know him through these last ten days, and now he had been taken away from me. And I loved him! I realized how much I loved him! I started screaming and crying as I drove. "God, why did you have to take him? Why did he have to go, Father? Why did he die?" I was crying to God saying, "Thank you, thank you that you are perfect. You know why this happened!" This controversy raged within me. "God, why?" and on the other hand, "Thank you, God! Thank you, God! It is your perfect will. Thank you, God, thank you! Comfort my mother. Comfort her!"

I was praying and crying, crying and praying, passing through one green light after another until I arrived at the hospital. I parked the car and rushed up the stairs to the oncological department. There I found my uncles, aunts, and cousins, but my mother was not there! They said to me, "Do you know?"

"Yes, I do. My father has died." No one had told me, but I knew it, because God Almighty had shown me. "Where is he?"

"You cannot go into the room. He's all covered. He's dead."

"Where is he?" I asked again. They saw that it was better not to argue with me, but to show me where he was.

"It's just here, the second room to the right. But he's all covered."

"That's all right," I said. I was still hoping that God would raise him from the dead.

As I was walking into the room, someone said — I don't remember who it was — "The nurses were surprised, because after you left last night he became very peaceful. He slept well and didn't have to take any medicine for pain. It was as if some sort of peace completely fell over him. Even when he died, he died in complete peace, with none of the excruciating pain that he had had before. It was as if something happened within him that caused him to be at peace."

As I looked at the person talking to me, I knew that that peace had fallen because God Almighty had caused my dad to accept the Messiah, even though he was unconscious. I knew that my God in heaven would not fail me! I had prayed for my father's salvation, "Lord, do not allow him to die unless he is saved."

My Father in heaven had answered my prayer. The peace that fell over my daddy was the peace of God Almighty, who is called "The Lord our peace." The good news of Yeshua, the Messiah who takes away the sins of the world, is called the gospel of peace. The miracle above all miracles, the miracle of salvation, had happened in my father's heart.

I went into the room. He was covered with a sheet. I shut the door, took out the psalms of David and began to scream aloud, and to speak aloud the Psalms of David. "The lord is my shepherd. I shall not want. Even though he takes me through the valley of the shadow of death, I will fear no evil,..." and on and on.

I preached to myself. I preached to my late dad the Psalms of David, just as I had when he was alive. That was my goodbye to my father, and I released him to go. I said, "God, thank you. Thank you that you've taken him at the right time."

And I left the room.

Chapter 24

Spiritual Warfare!

My father's funeral was on Tuesday. Carolina, Vivi, my mom and I rose early in the morning. Natalia came from the kibbutz, and we all got dressed and were ready to go to the funeral. I was hugging my mom, telling her how much I loved her, how much I would be with her. Whatever it would take, I would stay close to her to help her through this time as much as I could.

My mother was broken. She was very frail. Carolina was inconsolable. She had had the best relationship with my father, being the youngest. She was the one who had been at home most of the time, even after her teen years, and had bonded with my dad in a special way that none of us had. Vivi was strong, cool and collected. She was not showing any signs of breakdown.

And I was very, very sad about the death of my father, but I was sad in a healthy way. I knew my Father in heaven had caused me to cry in a healthy way, grieving for my dad without holding back any emotion, but also releasing him into his heavenly abode.

That morning as I woke up, the Holy Spirit of God had told me that I was to be dressed in white for the funeral. That was peculiar, because in Israel one is to dress in black.

But I obeyed God, because I knew he was saying, "Your dad is in heaven with me, so this is to be a time of rejoicing for you. There is no reason for you to be dressed in black. You'll be different." Besides, I sensed that God was telling me, "I've sanctified you and made you holy. I've made you white through the blood of my Son. Therefore you are white, and you will stay white in the midst of all the people."

This would be the first time that many people had seen me for almost a year. But they had heard all sorts of rumors concerning my tragic history.

We all boarded the car for the slow funeral procession and then walked toward the big hole in the ground. There my father would be lowered into the grave with no coffin, according to the tradition of the Jews, "From dust you've come, and to dust shall you return." The voice of the rabbi began preaching the last sermon of the funeral and chanting the Kaddish of the funeral.

My mother began crying, and I cried. My sister Vivi kept herself strong, and Carolina cried. The people in the audience started sobbing. Many people loved my dad dearly. He was a special man, a brilliant man, one who had a lot to give to the world with his knowledge of science.

Danny came to the funeral also. He was holding the hands of both my sisters and me, being very sweet and kind, something I hadn't seen in him for a long time. This was very good for me. I sensed that it was a present from God.

At the end, when the preaching ended, one of my sisters read a very special letter written about my dad. Then we began taking some of the earth around, and little stones, and putting them on the fresh grave. Tradition is that stones are to be put on the grave. I didn't know why the tradition said that, but that's what people do at Jewish funerals. Once I heard an explanation from a rabbi who said that the stones represent a new foundation for life. That death is not final but we should continue building and living even after someone has died.

"Yes!"

Another explanation said that the stones were put instead of flowers in order to differ from the way that the Christians adorn their tombs.

The funeral had ended, and people were slowly walking back to their cars. It was a most imposing, beautiful funeral — if a funeral can be called beautiful. It was a majestic event. People loved my dad.

As we were going back to the cars, the meditation group leader and the channeler who received messages from the masters in the heavenlies came up to me. "Ronit," she said, "I'm so happy to see you. You look so well. The prayers that we've prayed for you have really succeeded. We've sent you the light! You look so good, so full of light."

Indignation welled up within me! These people had been praying for me? These people, who represent demonic strongholds! These people, whose masters in the heavens are demons! These people who are into witchcraft and the occult, had been praying for me? And she had the nerve to tell me I looked good because of their prayers! Witchcraft had been my downfall. Meditation and yoga had been my downfall.

Dressed all in white, with my white hat, indeed I looked very good. But I turned back to her and said, "Dear lady, I owe my health and my life to Yeshua the Messiah of Israel, and to no one else. But I thank you for your love anyway." She shut up! She was totally shocked. I turned away, and left the place, indignant.

My Uncle Eleazar from Jerusalem came to me and asked, "Why are you dressed in white? You should be dressed in black."

"Uncle," I replied, "I know where my father is, and therefore I am dressed in white."

People were watching, listening, and criticizing me, but I didn't care. I knew who was with me at the funeral. I knew that Yeshua the Messiah of Israel was standing by my side at the funeral, comforting me and comforting my mother and my sisters. I knew it was true because he said, "I will never leave you. I will never forsake you."

We got in our cars and returned home. According to the tradition there would now be a period of seven days of mourning, but because this was just before the Passover, the time had to be shortened to three days. Holy days always take precedence over any type of funeral in Israel among the Jewish people, according to biblical tradition.

During the next three days there would be people coming and going, bringing food to the house. My mother would be allowed to mourn and wail and cry, remembering my dad and mourning in any way that she wished. When we got home I was ready to help, to bake and cook, greet the guests, and do whatever was needed to go through this time. We were all very sad.

But a surprise was awaiting me on arrival home. My mom came to me and said, "Andrea, please, —" she still wasn't used to my new name, Dominiquae — "Andrea, please tend to the people. My very close friends and I want to go into the room and spend some time together in meditation."

I exclaimed, "Mother!" I knew what she was going to do was wrong and displeasing to God.

"Don't worry about it," she said. "Just tend to the guests." She turned, and left the room.

The Spirit of God rose up in me in indignation! I knew what they would be doing, and it was confirmed later, when they talked about it. This whole group, her most favorite and personal friends, were immediately trying to contact the dead spirit of my father! And they contacted it, or something that they thought was it.

They now caused my mother to become subject to what was thought to be the spirit of my father, who would now be the master guide over her. Not God Almighty, not Yeshua the

Messiah of Israel, not the Way, the Truth, and the Life, but a spirit from among the dead.

In the Bible it is clearly written, "You shall not suffer a sorceress to live." It is written so clearly that mediums and channelers are an abomination to God and that contacting dead spirits is an abomination to God. Yet when my father's grave was still fresh — the very day that the funeral was held — they were already trying to contact him to become a spirit guide to my mom.

Oh, my heart was throbbing and I cried out, "O my God Almighty!" I began rebuking the devil in our house and rose up in warfare against the powers of darkness that were holding my mother and sisters captive. I was indignant, furious in my spirit, but I knew one thing: my best weapon was prayer and praise and love. I was going to use that weapon against the devil that had held my mom captive for so long.

I tended to the guests that kept arriving, who talked about my dad, saying so many nice things. There was an atmosphere of peace in the living room where I was waiting on them, because I had filled the place with prayer and I knew that the God of Israel was with me.

At the same time, I was aware that in two different rooms of the same house, two different things were happening. In one room, the devil was honored through the channeling and contacting of dead spirits, while in the living room God Almighty, the God of Israel, Yeshua Messiah was honored. There was a battle going on right in that house between good and evil, between God and the devil.

I was in the bathroom brushing my hair. It was the last day of mourning, the "sitting down for the dead." The Passover was about to begin. Suddenly a deep spirit of grief fell upon me and I said, "My God! Is Danny really to become my husband again?" I had been indoctrinated that I should be reconciled with my ex-husband. "If he really is to be my husband again, why hasn't he come to this time of 'sitting down for the dead'?"

It is customary for husbands to be with their wives when the wife's father dies. "Yes, he came to the funeral, Lord, but he has not been with me since. He has not come to the house, but he has let me grieve all by myself. If he is indeed my husband, why hasn't he come?"

God spoke to me and said, "Dominiquae, I want you to go down to the garden. I want to speak to you."

I obeyed God's Holy Spirit, went down to the garden and sat underneath the fragrant branch of a tree blooming with pink flowers. As I sat there, the voice of the Holy Spirit said, as clear as water, "Dominiquae, Danny is not your husband."

He said it so strongly that it shocked me. I began crying and asked in astonishment, "He's not my husband?"

I felt as if that day I had been widowed from him. It wasn't a divorce that I had gone through, but I was widowed. I felt like a widow! I began crying, both for my late father, and for Danny as if he was my late husband. I cried and cried and cried. (Little did I know then that in four years time Danny would take his life due to his illness and his constant resistance to forgive and to accept God's forgiveness through Yeshua.)

Then I said, "Okay, God, if Danny is not my husband, then Lord, am I ever going to marry again? Am I ever going to be able to fulfill the dream of having a family, with harmony and peace, and children?"

All my life I had been pursuing the goal of a family, peace and harmony, with children, in a wonderful marriage. I had never succeeded. "Am I ever going to marry again, Lord? And if I don't marry again, that's all right with me. I'll stay celibate, and I'll serve you. I will be content to be just your servant, like a nun."

"Yes!"

The voice of God's Holy Spirit came very clearly to my heart again as he said, "Dominiquae, you will never marry again."

As he said that, something broke within me. Even though I wanted so much to have a happy family, to show that it truly was possible to have a wonderful marriage in Israel, I said, "God, that's all right. I bless you, God. I thank you, Father that I will not marry again. I will serve you as a celibate. I will be a servant of God."

But then, the distinctive voice of my Father in heaven spoke to me sternly and strongly again, full of love yet full of authority. He said, "Dominiquae, you will never marry again, but you will marry for the first time, for the first time in Messiah, in Christ."

Ahhhhh! I was awed, and could hardly breathe as I said, "Lord, do you mean — that everything I have done until now is absolutely erased from my record, and I am entitled to a fresh new start?"

God's Holy Spirit seemed to agree with me. He reminded me that the Bible says in 2 Corinthians 5:17 that when we come to Christ, we become a new creature in Christ. The old has gone away, and the new has come. God showed me that I was a virgin in his eyes, ready to start a new life as if I'd never been married. Now I had all the possibilities and hope of finding a perfect husband, the one God had intended for me all along.

I began rejoicing at the same time that I was crying over the spiritual death of my ex-husband. I knew that God really had plans for my life, and that some of these plans one day included marriage to someone who believed in God and walked with Yeshua. It would be someone especially prepared for me, and I for him. I knew that this time, it would be a godly marriage that would hold, because God Almighty would put it together.

"Yes!"

I rose up from the garden fresh and new, ready to fight the world. I knew that my Father in heaven had heard my supplication. He knew the desire of my heart to establish a strong home in Israel.

Chapter 25

Baruch

"Mom, it's time for me to leave," I told her. "I need to go on."

"That's all right; if you feel you have to leave, Andrea. You've been here with us for two months now, and if you need to find your own place, I release you. And," she added, "I'll help you. I'll come help you to clean it."

The Lord had supplied a wonderful little apartment for me. I had prayed for it while still in England, and depicted it on a postcard to Adi. I had written, "Adi, God is going to give me a little house that will have a yard with fruit trees and a place where we can put a swing. The swing will not be in it, but there will be a place for it. That will be our sign that this is the place from God."

I found the place in a miraculous way, and it was exactly as I had depicted it to Adi. When I showed her the house I said, "Adi, do you see exactly what I showed you in the postcard, when I said God was going to give us this and that? Now God has done just that, a home only 20 minutes away from where you live. It has fruit trees in the yard and a place for a swing, but there's no swing in it yet."

Adi was delighted. "Mommy, yes! God has answered your prayers."

"*Yes!*"

This home was to be a house of prayer, a house for God. I thought that God would keep me there for a long time, but I didn't know. I only knew one thing — that if he kept me there for a few months, or for a few years, I would honor him in everything I did. Every room in that house would be dedicated to God.

The house had only a little furniture in it. I didn't even have enough dishes, so my mom lent me a few things, and then kept her promise to come and help me clean.

The very first week after I moved I said, "God, I really need somebody to help me move some things I left in Jerusalem, where I was before travelling to England." I had left my guitar, my radio-tape player, a table, and some other things that I really needed. "Lord, thank you," I said, "for helping find someone to bring my things back — someone who has a big van."

I prayed, and asked my brothers and sisters in the Lord about it, but no one seemed to have enough time to help. This was strange, because everyone helped everyone in this congregation, but no one had time to help me.

I was getting frustrated. I was visiting the Baptist village east of Tel Aviv, near Petah Tikvah one day. Our congregation used to have its Saturday meetings there. A brother in the Lord there, a very special, sensitive man of God, came to me and said, "Dominiquae, why are you striving so much to find someone to help bring your things from Jerusalem? If you just call Baruch, he'll help you."

I turned around and said, "Baruch who?"

"Baruch Bierman, you know."

The moment I heard his name I remembered an incident that had happened to me before I left for England. I jumped back and said "Baruch Bierman? No! I will not call that man!"

He looked at me perplexed. "But Dominiquae, why wouldn't you call him? He helps everybody."

"Yes!"

As he said, "He helps everybody," my heart softened a bit toward Baruch Bierman. I thought that if he helps everybody, he might not be so bad after all. "All right," I said. "Give me his telephone number."

I called his number, and heard a message on his answering machine. "Hello, Shalom. This is the house of Baruch Bierman. Please leave a message after the beep."

"Hello, Shalom," I said. "This is Dominiquae here. I don't know if you remember me, but you met me six months ago in the Central BusStation of Jerusalem. I need you to help me bring some of my things from Jerusalem to the Sharon Valley area. I would appreciate it if you would call me," and I gave my number.

As I hung up, the memory of what had happened six months before at the Central Bus Station flooded over me. I had just been born again. I was still very frail, but at the same time full of the Spirit of God and full of power and strength and happiness in God. It was the Feast of Tabernacles, and during that Feast I'd met lots of new people in the Lord.

These new friends and I were having a wonderful stroll down to the Central Bus Station of Jerusalem. Just as we arrived, a man appeared. He had a big beard and looked pretty threatening. He spoke to the people I walked with, these Christians who had just come from the celebration of the Feast of Tabernacles. After he heard a few things from them he said to me, "Welcome, Sister!" and he hugged me so hard he almost crushed all my bones!

He startled me because his rejoicing was so effusive, so expressive, and I was still so frail. In a way I was still afraid of men. I was taken aback, and looked at him. He had this tremendous wild beard. He seemed like a John the Baptist right in the middle of Jerusalem, full of muscles.

I said, "Yes, thank you. What is your name?"

"My name is Baruch, and I'm also a believer in Messiah. I'm so happy to see you, and to know you've come to know

"Yes!"

Yeshua the Messiah. Oh, how wonderful!" He kept on talking to me and began telling me everything about his life.

I didn't know the man from Adam, and here he was already telling me everything about his life! My heart was cold toward him, and I said to God, "God, this is one of those men I don't ever want to meet again. He's so rowdy and boisterous. Lord, thank you that I'll not meet this man again!"

This was Baruch Bierman! His muscles bulged because he had been installing air-conditioning with a hammer and chisel through concrete walls. He used to be a weight-lifter, and became born again in a tremendous way that I would learn of later on. He was a very strong man, kind of rough, but with a heart of gold, rather like a big teddy bear.

At that time the only thing I saw was that massive beard, and those muscles, — a man that was overwhelming. I had said, "God, I don't ever want to meet this man again!" And here I found myself dialing his number and leaving a message on his answering machine to help me bring my things from Jerusalem.

Adi and Yuval were playing in the room with me. It was already four o'clock. I'd been able to see them nearly every day all week, and had brought them home with me every weekend. We were bonding together and loving each other as if we'd never been separated. I'd gotten a plastic swimming pool where they could splash in the water as much as they wanted. I would teach them things, and we would praise and worship the Lord with worship tapes. We had such good times together.

Now here I was, waiting for this man, Baruch Bierman, to bring my things back from Jerusalem, and I was a little concerned. Danny, the children's father, would be coming any minute to pick them up, and Baruch would be coming any minute to bring my things.

Suddenly, a knock on the door! I opened it, and here was a man clean-shaven, very handsome, well dressed, who said, "I brought your things back from Jerusalem."

"Are you Baruch Bierman?"

"Yes, I am. Hello, Dominiquae, I'm happy to see you."

I was puzzled. The man looked so handsome and clean-shaven, well-kept, and well-groomed. So I said, "Are you the same man I met six months ago?"

He laughed. "Yes, I'm the same man, but God has taken my beard away from me. I was hired to manage a Wendy's restaurant, and the only condition for my hiring was that I would shave off my beard. I prayed about it and felt that God was releasing me to shave off my big beard."

"Oh my goodness," I told him. "You look so much better!"

He laughed again. "Come on, we've had a puncture in one of the tires. Let's see if we can get all your things into the house, before I get it fixed."

At that very moment, Danny arrived! I introduced Baruch to Danny, and Danny to Baruch. They seemed to get along all right, so I went out and started bringing things back into the house.

Danny just said, "Ronit (he refused to call me by my new name), I've come to take the children, because it's nearly their bedtime."

"Sure, no problem." I kissed Adi and Yuval good night, hugged them and said, "I'll see you tomorrow." Off they went with their daddy to their home.

Baruch came into the house with all my stuff, and then sat down on one of my chairs by the table. We began having the most delightful conversation! And this man, about whom I had said, "Oh God, I hope I never see him again!" had become a handsome, attractive man in my eyes.

He told me how he was saved, an awesome story. He had been behind bars in prison, when Yeshua the Messiah of

Israel appeared to him in full length. He could see his face, his nose, and his very Jewish features. For the first time in his life he realized that Yeshua was Jewish! This was not a Gentile Messiah as he had thought, but a Jewish Messiah.

"Dominiquae," he told me, "I was a mean person. I hated everybody, but when Yeshua touched me and came into my life, as I read his word and read the New Testament, love hit me. All hate melted away. The truth of God's word set me free to love people.

"Now," he added, "when I pray for people and lay hands on them, I have the compassion of God. I feel their hurts in my own body. Then I touch them, and they are miraculously healed."

As Baruch was telling me how God saved him, from prison and from hate, and brought him back to the land of the Jewish people and to Jerusalem," I started crying. Tears were streaming down my face, for God had touched my heart for this man.

"Baruch," I said when he finished the story of his conversion, "would you mind coming back after seven tonight? We're going to have a special meeting with our congregation, to dedicate my house to the Lord. Would you mind joining us?"

Baruch smiled and said, "Sure. I love dedicating houses to the Lord. I'll be here."

"Right now," I said, "I need to do some errands. I'll be back later on."

He hugged me goodbye, and went away. This time I was not in the least overwhelmed by his hug. I hugged him back, giving him a holy hug as a friend, and then he left and went his way.

I was so happy! I knew that this man who had come into my life was a special one, someone who would be a real friend for me.

"Yes!"

As I was preparing the house for the dedication that evening, I knew this would be a good meeting. The only thing I hadn't taken into consideration was that I didn't have enough glasses for everyone. But I knew God would make up for my lack.

Slowly, slowly, people began arriving. They would knock on the door, come in, and settle down in the front room. Tony and Orna came. Everyone in the congregation who was available that night came. We began singing, to praise and worship God.

While we were singing, Baruch, a little late, arrived and sat down among us, handing me a present. They were brand new glasses, exactly what I needed for my guests that night! It was as if God's Holy Spirit had talked to him and said, "Baruch, she needs glasses, so please buy some for her." He had brought them as a special house-warming present.

Chapter 26

A New Congregation In Israel!

Ring-ring! Ring-ring! I dashed to the phone in my little home. Baruch was on the line.

"I am considering having a business here in Jerusalem, in a weight-lifter's place. It will be a kind of health corner with fruit juices for the people who exercise. Would you be willing to give me some of your expertise concerning this place, and see whether it would be a good investment for me?"

"Sure, I'd be happy to help you. Actually, I happen to be going to Jerusalem tomorrow, and I can meet you next to the main store in the center of Jerusalem."

"Okay, no problem." We decided on a time to meet, and hung up.

The following day I took a bus to Jerusalem and went to the appointed place. He was not there, so I sat down to read my Bible. I did this whenever I had time available. I would open the scriptures and refresh myself in the word of God, and talk to God.

I was startled to hear a man say, "You're having a honeymoon with Yeshua, aren't you?" I looked up and saw it was Baruch.

"Yes," I said, "indeed I am in a honeymoon period with him. I love God with all my heart. But somebody has already told me this honeymoon will end very soon."

Baruch answered passionately, "I rebuke those words! In the name of Yeshua, you will not finish your honeymoon with Yeshua! It is going to continue with him for your entire lifetime!"

Was I ever happy for his words! He had been saved for the past ten years and was walking with God. He knew many more things than I concerning the faith, and its ups and downs.

We took a bus to the place where Baruch planned to rent space for his fruit juice stand and health food corner. Before entering, we prayed and said, "Lord, show us if this is from you." Then we went in.

As soon as we had gone in I felt that it was not a business that God had appointed for him. I sensed in the Spirit that he should not invest any money in it. So as we came out onto the walkway I said, "Baruch, I don't think this is for you. I think you should drop the matter."

He accepted my counsel. But then I said, "I have a surprise for you. I can invite you to lunch, for free."

"Oh? That sounds exciting. No one would turn away an offer for a free lunch, would they?"

"I have a special place where I'm going to take you," I said. "I'm a tour guide, and I have a discount and special treatment as a tour guide in a place called The Promenade. It is actually a restaurant that overlooks Old Jerusalem, a place where people go to have an overview of the city. I have a friend in the restaurant who is also a tour guide, and he gives special treatment to those of us who are tour guides, so that we'll bring tour groups to his restaurant. So — God has provided it, let's use it!"

Baruch was really happy about the idea. We went to the parking lot where he had left his truck. It was a Volkswagon, double-cabin truck. It was an ugly green. I sat in the truck, blessed that it would take us every place we had to go, in spite of its ugly green color, because it was a very sturdy vehicle.

We arrived at the Promenade and found two seats outside on the terrace, overlooking beautiful Jerusalem. As we shared experiences in the Lord, an idea came to me. "Baruch, I have a request for you."

"What is it?"

"I have a brother who's been in different mental institutions for the last nine years, and he's accepted the Lord. I preached the gospel to him and he was saved. But he has never walked with God, and he still doesn't understand how he can be Jewish and Messianic at the same time." I felt that the Lord had told me Baruch had a key that would really help my brother, Ariel. "Would you please pray about the possibility of coming with me to the mental hospital and ministering to him?"

Baruch said very sternly, "No, I will not pray about it!"

Oh, my heart sank, for I had really hoped that he would come.

"I have nothing to pray about," Baruch explained. "The Bible says I should go visit those in the hospital. So when are we going?"

I was so happy! I knew that something would touch Ariel, because Baruch has a special gift from God to help Jewish people who cannot understand how to become Messianic, receiving Yeshua as Messiah, and still be Jewish.

We were sitting under a tree in the garden of the mental institution. Ariel was sitting with us. We had come all the way to Hadera, which is between Tel Aviv and Haifa. Baruch was opening the Scriptures to Ariel, explaining things to him. Baruch had opened to Isaiah 53, showing Ariel how Jesus was "bruised for our transgressions and pierced for our iniquities. The chastisement of our peace was upon him, and through his stripes we are already healed."

He explained to Ariel how the Messiah is revealed in the Tanach (the Old Testament), in the different books, and by the different prophets. Then he opened to Proverbs 30 and said, "Do you see? 'Who has gone up to heaven, and who has come down? What is the name of his son? Would you know?' Ariel, do you know the name of the Son of God, the one who has gone up, and come down? Who is the one who arose from the dead?"

Ariel said, "Yeshua the Messiah!" His eyes were opened! Ariel's eyes were opened! He could understand! "Yes," he exclaimed, "my Bible, the Tanach, says this is the Messiah. It is God's son!"

Then Baruch opened the Bible to Isaiah 9 and read, "'Unto us a child is born, unto us a son is given, and the government is upon his shoulders. And he will be called... the Everlasting Father, the Prince of Peace.'"

"Ariel, who is this child that was born? Who was the son that was given, the one who was called 'the wonderful Counselor, the mighty God, the everlasting Father, the Prince of Peace?' Who is the one who was not only his son but was also the mighty God?"

Ariel exclaimed, "The Son of God, Yeshua the Messiah of Israel!" From that moment my brother would start a process of healing from his mental problems by the power of the God of Israel! I was helping Baruch read those Scriptures in Hebrew to Ariel when I happened to look up. People were streaming toward us from all over the hospital! Some of their faces were distorted. They were under drug treatment, but they were streaming toward us. We felt as if we were in the midst of the Sermon on the Mount, when Jesus was preaching and the masses were listening. Here we were surrounded by a sea of different people in need of God!

That day a new church, a new congregation of Messianic believers was birthed in Israel, right in the heart of that mental institution. Hidden from the eyes of doctors, we came every week to minister to them, and God would add to the numbers. People were being saved and miraculously set free from their mental illnesses by the anointing of the Holy Spirit.

Not once were we stopped. Not once did the doctors know that under their very noses people were being healed of insanity, of depression, of hearing different voices. They were being set free by the mighty power of God.

We didn't know then that very soon we would be discovered and that the door would be closed. No longer would its people be ministered to for salvation and healing. The ministry would not be allowed to continue.

But God is almighty, and he allowed us for a season to taste of what he could do for people whose situations were desperate.

Chapter 27

The Letter Of The Law

I had been struggling with my emotions for the last three months. I remembered the day when the Lord had said, "Dominiquae, I'm taking you up to Jerusalem for the purpose of marriage."

The only man I knew in Jerusalem was Baruch, so I believed from this that God had been speaking to me about marrying Baruch, but I was so, so afraid!

"O my God," I prayed, "perhaps this is my imagination. I don't ever want to marry a man again and end up in divorce. O God, I want to make sure this is of you!" I was in an emotional turmoil.

I had gone to my mom's house that day, and she had asked, "Andrea, are you in love with Baruch?"

"Of course not, mother! We are only friends."

My mother looked at me with a very peculiar expression in her eyes, as if to say, "You can say you're only friends, but I can tell there's something else going on here."

Throughout these last three months Baruch and I had grown very close to each other. We were spending almost day and night together. Well, in the night he would go to his friends' house nearby to sleep, because as believers of course we would not be sharing a house or a room together. We would not be having an extra-marital relationship because it does not honor God and is forbidden in the scriptures. So we were sanctified in our bodies and would not give any room to the devil to try to steal our purity from us.

But for many days throughout the week Baruch would spend time with me. He found a job in construction near where I lived, even though his home was in Jerusalem. He found a couple of families who were friends where he could stay the night, Rimona and Ephraim, Miriam and Raviv.

Baruch and I became prayer partners. We would pray together, and then go to the mental institution to minister to the mentally ill.

One day we came to the house meeting where Tony my pastor was. Tony was aware of what was happening in the mental institution and was excited about it. "Baruch and Dominiquae," he said, "give us a report about what is going on in the mental institution."

"Well Tony," I answered, "we went there again this last Tuesday. We preached the gospel, and three more people were saved and we blessed them with cookies, and...."

Tony looked at me and said, "What is this 'we, we, we' business? It seems to me you're together all the time." Tony had begun worrying about this. As a dear brother in the Lord and the pastor of this congregation, he was very concerned for me. I was happy for his protection, as I didn't want to make any more mistakes.

******

Baruch and I were going up to Jerusalem to visit some friends of his, driving in his truck — that ugly, green truck that was such a blessing to us.

"Baruch, my mother asked me a very peculiar question today."

"What did she ask you?"

"Well, she asked me if I was in love with you."

Baruch perked up, looked over at me and asked, "What did you tell her?"

"I told her no, of course. I explained that we are only friends."

Baruch turned pale and became completely silent, not saying a word. After a while as we continued driving on he began talking about something very banal, about a chocolate cake. "Oh man," he said, "I have the most amazing, amazing recipe for a chocolate cake. The truth is, whoever makes me that chocolate cake, I'm going to fall in love with her, because it is the best chocolate cake I've ever tasted. That's the way to my heart."

Well, being a nutritionist, chocolate cake wasn't one of the best things I wanted to bake for anyone. But I was a little more flexible in my principles concerning food than in more important matters, so I said, "Baruch, don't be so dramatic. I'm your friend and I know how to bake. Just give me your fabulous recipe and I'll bake it for you. You don't have to fall in love with me for that."

Baruch quickly pulled over to the side of the road without any advance warning, stopped the truck dead cold, turned around and faced me. "It is too late, Dominiquae, because I'm already in love with you!"

Oh my! I had just said to my mother that I don't love the man. I really didn't mean to say that, but I had to guard my heart because I didn't want to fall in love again. Falling in love meant real trouble for me! Yet God had been speaking to me, saying that Baruch was to be my husband. I knew it was the voice of God, but I was terrified.

I looked back at this man with a heart of gold. He was sometimes very rough and gruff, but I saw his eyes full of tears, and full of love. I said quietly, "I guess I'm in love with you, too."

Baruch had doctrines which did not allow him to marry me. He did not believe he was allowed to marry a divorcee. He would say that time and again, but would add, "What can I do? I'm in love with you, and I cannot marry you."

One day I got very indignant with him. "Baruch, if I am good enough for God, I am good enough for you. The Bible says that I am a new creation. I am allowed to have everything that was in the past taken away. I have been given a completely new life. God told me that I would be marrying for the first time in the Messiah, that I am not a divorcee any more. It's a spiritual thing that God has done. He's entitled me to start a new life as if I'd never had any other marriage."

Baruch was listening. "Yes, yes, but I need to understand it from the Bible myself."

******

Baruch decided to go to a monastery, to fast and pray for three days and seek God concerning our marriage. He really wanted to hear from God, even though he already loved me very much.

During that time I went back to my mother's house and found that there were a few objects that I had left behind, and a box or two of jewelry. I decided to bring these things home with me.

I had used a few of the things during my stay in Eilat, some necklaces and earrings. There was even a suitcase with things in it for a type of gambling game, and some of the cards I had used for palm reading. I brought all these objects back with me to go through. I expected to throw some out, but to leave intact some of the jewelry.

I was really ignorant. Before I knew it, I had a terrible headache. I hated myself. I hated the house where I was. The atmosphere in the house changed completely. I wanted to die! I felt terrible. I didn't know what to do and I decided to call our friends Miriam and Raviv.

"Please come over," I pleaded. "Baruch has left for three days and I feel so terrible I don't know what I can do. I want him to come back. I'm feeling horrible!"

I was not myself! They came over and prayed for me, but they never realized what the problem was. I didn't realize it either.

Before I knew it, by the third day since Baruch had left, I was totally wiped out. I couldn't do anything at all! I felt absolutely strangled! I couldn't move. I was in terrible confusion, lying on my sofa unable even to get up. I felt like I had to run away from this place!

The only thing I managed to understand from the Lord as I was praying was that Baruch would come back by Sunday.

On Saturday, Baruch came back. He came into the house, and the first thing I said was, "Baruch, please get me out of here. I hate this home!"

Baruch was amazed, because he knew I loved my little home. The presence of God was there all the time. He said, "Dominiquae, what is the matter with you?"

"Don't worry about it. Just take me out. Take me out of here, quickly! I can't stay here one minute longer!"

He took me out, and we went away from the place. He began sharing all that had happened during his last three days. Then I began telling him about the things I had brought from my mother's, and that some of them were things that had been used during my times of witchcraft in Eilat.

Baruch suddenly perked up. He said, "You did what!"

And I said, "Well, I brought them home and I have them there."

Baruch looked at me astounded and grabbed my hand. "Come home, immediately! Come back with me!" He pulled

"Yes!"

me into the car and drove me back home. As we went in he asked, "Where are these things?"

I showed him the plastic box, and the little cases, and the jewelry, and —.

"Get rid of these things!" he exclaimed. "They need to be burned!"

"What? Why?" I said.

"Because," he said, "these things are accursed objects! These are objects of witchcraft! You've used them in the occult! They have a spiritual influence on you, and they've been poisoning you, and poisoning your house!"

Oh my! I struck my forehead and I said, "How true! It's since I've brought them over that I've wanted to die! I haven't been able to do anything! I felt terribly oppressed, strangled, and the whole atmosphere of my house changed."

Baruch said, "That's what it is! These are accursed objects. You're not to have these objects! Let's make a fire and burn them!"

I was only too happy to do that. He took them all out. He burned them, with revulsion watching them burn. Then he rebuked every demonic stronghold and spirit that they may have left behind.

After we had done that, cleansing the house with prayer and praise and worship, the atmosphere of God was restored to the house and I was totally set free from that oppression.

From that day onward, I learned one lesson. Everyone needs to be very careful what objects are brought into the house. Some of them are accursed objects, without our knowing it. Sometimes Jews and Christians have objects in their home that bring curses, for example, things like different figures and statues they bring home from other countries. Some of these are symbols of false gods, and they are accursed objects. They have been used in pagan worship or in witchcraft.

I learned that in the house of a believer there should be no accursed objects but only blessed objects, objects that can give glory to God. I paid a price of three days of heaviness and oppression for that, but I learned a big lesson.

That evening our little congregation was gathered in the home of one of the members. One of our dearest friends, one who always provided hospitality for Baruch when he was in the area in order to be near me, Ephraim, was preaching that night. Suddenly he spoke a very peculiar sentence that had nothing to do with what he was preaching about! He said, "The letter of the law kills, but the Spirit gives life."

That sentence was engraved on Baruch's mind and heart! At the same time, I left the meeting to go into the bathroom. It seems that God speaks to me in some of the most unlikely places, and one of them is the bathroom.

"Dominiquae," God said to me, "tomorrow at 8:30."

"Tomorrow at 8:30? What, God?"

He didn't answer me. He just gave me the time. I left the bathroom, went back into the meeting and sat down again.

At the close of the meeting, our pastor the leader came over to me. "Dominiquae, I want to speak with you." He looked very concerned. "Tomorrow morning, I'm going to come to your house with my wife, to talk with you about Baruch and your relationship with him."

"No problem. I'd be happy to have you, and to converse with you about this relationship."

"Very well then. We'll be there at 8 in the morning."

God had told me in the bathroom that something would happen at 8:30 so I though that perhaps he meant this — 8, 8:30, what's the difference?

I still had not learned that the God of Israel is very particular about his timings and his hours. "Sure," I told him. "I'll wait for you at 8 tomorrow morning."

He added, "I don't want Baruch to be there. I want you alone."

"*Yes!*"

"Sure. That's fine."

Morning came. Yuval had been over, sleeping with me. When the leaders came, Yuval ran out in the yard to play, as he loved to do.

They looked very serious, but they were friendly. They were dear to me and I valued their counseling deeply. They sat down, and he said, "OK, Dominiquae, let's start. Explain to me. What is your relationship with Baruch?"

In my heart I said, God, what am I going to tell the man now? I know that Baruch is in love with me and I'm in love with him, but his doctrines prevent him from marrying me. What can I tell him, Lord? Then, as if led by the Holy Spirit, I began telling Tony the whole story.

"Brother, I'm going to tell you the story from the beginning. Seven or eight months ago I met Baruch at the central station in Jerusalem. When I saw him for the first time, I said 'God, I don't want to ever see this man again!'"

On and on I told the story, how I came back from England and called Baruch to bring my things from Jerusalem. I told how we started going to the mental institution, where people were being saved and healed from their insanity, and how a little congregation was birthed in the center of that mental institution. I told him how my brother, Ariel, got saved, and I was telling the whole story without really answering his question directly. All the time I was praying in my heart for God to help me.

I had told Baruch the previous night that the congregational leaders were coming over. "Baruch, you'd better be interceding for me, because they're going to ask me about you and I have no idea what I can tell them."

"Yes," Baruch said, "I'm going to get up early and I'll be praying for you at 8 o'clock when they come over." Baruch was staying at the home of Rimona and Ephraim, the friend that had preached the previous night. At 8:29 I was still

"Yes!"

telling the leaders how our relationship had evolved, when all of a sudden I heard a commotion in the yard.

"Baruch! Baruch!" Yuval called excitedly. "Oh mommy, Baruch is here!" Yuval loved Baruch. He was his very good friend.

Baruch burst into the room where we were having this conversation. He said nothing, because he was breathing so hard. He was panting, winded, because he had run all the way from Ephraim and Rimona's house, five or ten minutes away, without stopping.

"Do you want some water, Baruch?" I asked.

He shook his head, no.

"Do you want some breakfast?"

Again he shook his head, no, still too breathless to answer.

These leaders were not happy to see him, because they didn't want him to have any effect on my answers concerning our relationship. They were afraid that he was taking advantage of me. They were very protective of me, and I was grateful.

Baruch was looking right at me, still unable to get his breath to speak. And suddenly I realized — it was exactly 8:30 in the morning! Someone had sent Baruch to me, and that someone was the Holy Spirit, but I didn't know why.

Baruch took a deep breath, pointed at me with his finger, and in the most dramatic fashion said, "Dominiquae, will you marry me?"

The peace of God fell on me, clothing me from head to toe. "Sure, I will marry you."

That was all. Baruch became very quiet. I turned my head back toward the leaders and said, "This is the answer to your question about our relationship."

They were not happy at all! They felt that this was too dramatic, and they left, very indignant.

"Yes!"

Baruch left too, just saying, "I'm leaving, and I'm not going to bother you anymore." He didn't even touch my hand or anything. "I'm coming to pick you up at 11 in the morning, and we are going to go buy you a diamond engagement ring, so be ready." And off he went.

My heart was leaping and rejoicing, but my pastors were not happy. This was not exactly the way they had intended this to happen! But, every one of us needs to learn that God has his ways for many things. For even the day before, God had spoken to me and said, "8:30, Dominiquae." He hadn't explained what he meant. And exactly at 8:30 Baruch asked me to marry him, and exactly at 8:30 I said, "Yes, I will."

Baruch and I spent many days in prayer and fasting for our pastors to agree that we were to get married. We didn't want to be married in rebellion. We wanted his blessing.

One day we went to his office, and I said to him in typical Israeli "Hutspah," which means with "a lot of nerve." "Brother," I said, "we are not going to leave your office until you give us your blessing for this marriage."

He felt embarrassed. "Well," he said, "Okay, let me pray for you." As he started praying the Holy Spirit completely took over his prayer and he gave us a wonderful blessing! It was then that he probably realized that God indeed had appointed us to be married.

A few days later God's Holy Spirit spoke to me. "Dominiquae, I want you to leave this home that I've given you." This house had been given to me in June and I had gotten engaged on the 31st of August, so I had spent three months here. Now the Lord was saying, "I want you to move on now. Go to Jerusalem and rent a little place near Baruch so you can be together throughout the engagement period. There are things I have to do, and I need you both in the same place. Baruch needs to go back to Jerusalem."

"All right, Lord. But if you have really spoken to me, I am asking you right now to make sure this house gets re-

"Yes!"

rented quickly, so that I don't need to put any effort into this. Then I'll know it's really you that has spoken."

Just as I had prayed, the first person that came to see the house rented it. The owners were happy to let me go because I left everything in order and had paid all my bills. Only God could have convinced me to move, for it had been such a wonderful place of rest and peace for me. It had been a place near my children's home so that I could see them almost every day.

I knew that by going to Jerusalem, which is an hour and a half drive each way, I would not be able to see the children except perhaps on weekends. This was a sacrifice God was asking of me, but whatever my Lord asked of me, I would obey.

If I could not see my children as often, God would make up for it some other way. I owed him my life and every breath I took. Even if I could not see my dearly loved children as often, I would obey, and God would be my exceeding, great reward.

Chapter 28

Meeting My Destiny

It was the Feast of Tabernacles time in Jerusalem again. A whole year had gone by since the Lord had come into my life, and many things had happened. I was engaged to be married to the man God had prepared for me. My life was beginning to have some shape and form again.

But Baruch was out of work. He had an air-conditioning company, but no business was coming in, and we were faced with financial trials. The Lord was meeting our needs just day by day.

I needed to find a place to live. At the time I left my house, I was guiding a group of tourists for ten days, and I was provided with a hotel room every one of those days, but now I had to find a place to live.

A few days before, I had taken my tourists to the Wailing Wall. I had told them that they should write their petitions on a little piece of paper and put it in the cracks of the wall and the God of Israel would answer their prayers. There is a special anointing on that wall, because King Solomon had prayed, when he built the temple, " God, if anybody comes from a foreign land to this place and prays toward this temple, I'm asking you to answer him. Show yourself mighty and strong, and answer their prayers."

So all my tourists, who were Christians, wrote their requests and put them in the wall. Of course I didn't put my prayer request in because I could talk to God directly. It was such a simple thing to just write a prayer request and put it in the wall that I didn't want to do that!

But as they were writing their requests I was praying. "Lord," I said, "I've been praying for you to find a home for me. You told me to leave. You haven't provided for me yet. Please, provide a place for me before I finish this tour."

The voice of God came to me clearly. "Dominiquae, you do exactly what you told your tourists to do. Put your request on a little paper in the cracks of the wall, and I will answer your prayer."

This surprised me! But I said, "All right," and humbled myself before God, wrote my request on a scrap of paper, folded it and put it in a crack.

One day before the tour ended a woman advertised that she had a room for rent, just five minutes from where Baruch was living! He was living in a settlement on the way to Jericho from the desert of Judea, 15 or 20 minutes away from Jerusalem. The room was $100 a month, only a five minute walk to Baruch's. I rented it. God had answered my request tucked into the Wailing Wall.

******

"Go to the United States!" Baruch gasped. "What do you mean, God has spoken to you to go to the United States!"

"I sense that God is saying we're to go to Bible school at a place called Christ for the Nations," I tried to explain.

Baruch looked extremely serious. This doctrine that he had, — that all Jews were to return to the land of Israel — coursed through his mind. He said, "I believe that the devil is the only one that takes Jews away from the land of Israel. To America? And then back again?"

"Yes!"

Just then the peace of God overshadowed him and he said more thoughtfully, "Dominiquae, you are right. God is speaking to us to leave and study at this Bible school, Christ for the Nations."

"I had a vision, Baruch," I told him. "I saw ourselves traveling in a place where there were these big, black, volcanic-like mountains. We were very happy. I asked the Lord, 'Where are we?' and the Lord said, 'Hawaii.'"

"After that I had another vision, Baruch. I saw a revolving tower with a restaurant on top, and I knew we were to be in that city."

Baruch and I asked a brother in the Lord from the States about that. He said, yes, there was such a restaurant in a tower, in Dallas, Texas.

We were elated! In a supernatural way God had shown us we were to go to Hawaii and to Texas. But we didn't know whether Christ for the Nations was in Hawaii, or in Dallas.

I finished the last day of the tour and hurried to meet Baruch at the entrance of the building where the Feast of Tabernacles was to be held. What a difference between this year and last year at this time! Last year I was so frail and broken, yet full of God and full of hope. Now I was walking with God, full of the Word, full of strength, set free and healed in so many ways.

Baruch was half an hour late. While waiting I was praying, "Where is he, Lord? Where is he?"

"Just stay put," the Lord replied. "Stay right where you are."

I was next to a tree close to the entrance. The place was bustling with people coming and going, rejoicing and excited about the celebration to come. Suddenly I heard a woman speaking very loudly. She was wearing a long mumu and had a flower in her short hair. She was in her sixties, but looked younger.

She saw me and asked, "Do you need a ticket for the Feast of Tabernacles? Are you an Israeli?"

"Yes I am." I told her.

"Do you believe in the Messiah?"

"Yes I do."

"Oh, how wonderful!" she said. "You're Jewish?"

"Yes, I'm Jewish."

"You can have this ticket for the Feast of Tabernacles. I'll give it to you, free."

"Thank you, but my husband to be is about to come and he has tickets."

"Okay," she said. "Well, praise the Lord, thank you, no problem."

As she was leaving, the Holy Spirit impressed on me to call her back, ask her name and where she was from. "Excuse me, lady," I called. She turned around and I asked "Where are you from?"

"I'm from Hawaii.

Oh, my heart leaped within me — Hawaii! "What's you name?" I asked.

"My name is Mary Praise-the-Lord Adams."

Mary Praise-the Lord Adams had come into our lives. She was like a volcano waiting to erupt, full of the word of God, of the power of the Holy Spirit, of the joy of the Lord and full of maturity in God. She had the power to move mountains, power to pray that rain would fall, or rain would stop. Miracles followed her wherever she went, preaching the word of God. She was a true servant of the Lord, whom he now brought into our lives, and she became our chaperone. Mary Praise-the-Lord Adams was strategically placed in our path just at the time God had been speaking to us that it was time to leave Israel and go to the United States. She could tell us not only all about Hawaii, but also suggest some very basic principles of how we were to walk by faith in God.

"Yes!"

Walking by faith meant that we would have to trust God every minute of the day concerning our finances. Even when we saw that there was no way to pay our bills, we would rejoice and praise God, and our bills would be paid. Mary Praise-the-Lord Adams taught us to praise Him about everything. We'd heard about these things before, but we'd never had to live by them. She encouraged us, and we loved her!

Sometimes when Baruch and I were at his house, Mary Praise-the-Lord Adams would shout from her room, "You're too quiet down there! What are you doing?" She was a marvelous chaperone. She would certainly keep us holy until the day of our wedding!

One night she and I were both staying overnight at Baruch's. I didn't want to sleep there by myself, but with the two of us women it was fine. I was in the living room. Baruch was in his bedroom, and Mary Praise-the-Lord Adams in the guest room.

Suddenly I heard a commotion at about four in the morning. Baruch came out of his room with his face all twisted in pain saying, "Dominiquae, I can barely breathe! Help me! Pray for me! I'm dying!" And with that, he fell on the floor, and was no longer breathing.

As I looked at him I became absolutely peaceful. "What are you doing on the floor, Baruch? You are a man of faith! You should not be lying there!"

The fury and indignation of God rose within Baruch. He began beating his chest and started breathing again, commanding his heart to work, commanding the devil to take his hands off of him! Soon he was able to get on his feet, and began quoting Scripture to the devil who had tried to kill him, and to make his heart stop beating.

He had had a massive heart attack. He felt so strong after he had quoted Scripture to the devil that he decided, "This is it." God had healed him from the heart attack, and he would go to work as usual at his construction company. He had found a job in building and construction in the Israeli Parliament of the Israeli Knesset. After breakfast he grabbed his lunch and went out the door, full of passion and zeal to go to work that day.

I knew that God had done a tremendous miracle, but I didn't feel right about his going immediately back to work in building and construction. I felt impelled to follow him out the door, and then I saw Baruch completely prostrated on the walk, unable to continue walking even one more step.

He leaned heavily on me and we came back home. For two weeks, my future husband who was so strong and full of muscles, could not lift one chair. But he never went to a doctor or to a hospital, because he knew his total healing from a massive heart attack was to come only through prayer and the word of God.

Mary Praise-the-Lord Adams had faith for miracles. She laid her hands on him and prayed, "O Lord, don't even bother mending this old heart of his. Just give him a new one!"

God indeed gave him a new heart, for he became very strong again, as if he'd never had a heart attack before. He never touched medication, and no doctor treated him except Yeshua, the Messiah, the doctor, the healer of Israel.

These seven months of engagement were hectic for us. We learned to know each other in many ways. One of the most important things that happened was that all our jobs were cancelled. It was amazing! It didn't matter what we could do, for God would close door after door in the job situation.

We needed a lot of money for the wedding to be held on April 8. And we needed money for tickets to Hawaii and for the Bible school in the States. The Lord had shown us we were to work as volunteers for a few months in Hawaii with Youth With a Mission, and then go on to the Christ for the Nations Bible School in Dallas, Texas.

But we didn't have a dime coming in. Baruch, after the heart attack, could not work in construction any more, and his business endeavors shut down, for no customers came.

As a tour guide, I had lots of tour engagements. My diary was full of them, but one by one, each engagement was cancelled. It was becoming a joke! The phone would ring, "Hello? Is this Dominiquae?"

"Yes," I would say.

"Dominiquae, we have a group for you tomorrow. You will be guiding fifty people in French."

"Sure, no problem." I'd hang up the telephone.

Two minutes later the phone would ring again. "Hello, is this Dominiquae?"

"Yes, this is Dominiquae."

"Dominiquae, we're sorry, but the group that we told you about, the French group, has just cancelled, so you'll not be guiding tomorrow."

Situations like this occurred day after day, week after week, so that before we knew it, Baruch and I were totally out of work, and out of money!

In miraculous ways, the Lord would provide. One day God spoke to me as I was on a bus near the Tel Aviv airport. "Dominiquae," he said, "have you begun to sell all your possessions in order to leave?"

"No, Lord, I haven't," I admitted.

"What are you waiting for?" He asked.

When I got back home I said, "Baruch, God is telling me that we need to sell everything, and leave."

"Okay," he said.

We put all our things on sale, and as they were sold, we managed to live on the money week after week, month after month.

During those months of preparation for marriage and for Bible school, God's Holy Spirit visited me, and in a vision He took me to heaven.

"Yes!"

I was walking in heaven with the Son of God, Yeshua. We came to the edge of the heavenlies when suddenly Yeshua said, "Dominiquae, look down."

I looked down, and saw the earth. It was completely white! I remembered the scripture that says, "The fields are white unto harvest, but the laborers are few."

The Lord said, "Dominiquae, what are you seeing?"

"Well God, I'm seeing that the fields are white unto the harvest."

The Lord looked at me and said, "Dominiquae, you are called to the harvest. By that I mean that you are called to the mission field. You are called to go and find the lost for me. You are called to go and evangelize for me. You are called to do ministry for me."

I turned to the Lord and said, "But oh, God, what about Adi and Yuval? How can I leave them?"

Immediately the vision turned into another vision and I saw a big heart. Yeshua, the Son of God, was sitting in the middle of that heart, and he had each one of my two children on his knees. He said, "Dominiquae, I have them, but you must go."

I bowed down. I knelt before God Almighty. I agreed with him, that I would obey whatever he would say.

Little had I known that this is the road I had begun, when in the little room in England I had committed myself to be sent out, after listening to the tape of Derek Prince. "Who is willing to become an ambassador and work for the Lord?" he had asked.

I remembered how, in that room, I had stood up and said, "Lord, but what about my children?" But then I had put the tape on again, agreed with God, and said, "I trust you, Lord that you will take care of my children. I will do what you want me to do."

Now, on this day, I recommitted myself to God. I understood from the vision that I had a calling from God. I had to follow that calling, even if it hurt. God Almighty was to be first in my life. I believed to see many blessings come into the lives of my children, as I followed and obeyed my Lord.

When I shared with Baruch about the commitment that I had made before the Lord in England this is what he said: "Dominiquae, I was in that conference in Jerusalem when Derek Prince challenged the people to be sent out and become ambassadors for Him," he took a breath with excitement and awe, "and guess what?" he said. "What?" I was expectant, Baruch proceeded, "In spite of the opposition of my best friends, I went to the altar and committed myself with many others to be sent out to preach God's gospel!" So Baruch and I had made the same commitment before the Lord, in different parts of the world!

Chapter 29

The Ugly Green Truck

We were in the ugly green truck again. This time we were heading for the Dead Sea. Adi and Yuval were singing and rejoicing in the truck. I had promised them that we would go to the new water park that was right by the Dead Sea in the middle of the desert.

My two little children had accepted the Lord as their own personal Savior a few weeks earlier. This is how it happened. At the time I was caring for Matan and Raphael, the two children of a friend who was a believer, who had just had a new baby. I had brought Matan and Raphael to Baruch's apartment for him to look after. They were both very sweet children who had been born again. Adi and Yuval were also with me that weekend.

We had been in the bedroom together. I was having my time of prayer in the room while the four children played. "Okay, children," I said. "Now we are going to have a time of Bible study and prayer."

The four children had gathered around me and I began explaining about the fruit of the Holy Spirit, and how it matures within a believer's heart. "Let's play this little game," I told them. "Everyone should have the fruit of the Spirit. One is called love — let this be a banana. Another one is called joy — let that be an orange. Still another one is called peace — let this be grapes. Each of you grab one of these fruits and compare it to a natural fruit. Then let me know what you think about this fruit, in the natural, and in the spiritual."

As we were playing that game, I asked Matan and Raphael, "Do you know who is living in your heart?"

"Oh yes," they said. "We have the Spirit of God. We have Yeshua, the Son of God, living in our hearts."

I turned to Adi and Yuval. "Adi," I asked, "Do you have Yeshua living in your heart?"

"No, I don't," Adi said.

I turned to Yuval. "Yuval, do you have Yeshua, the Son of God, living in your heart?"

Yuval said, "No, mommy, I don't."

And I said to Adi and Yuval, "Do you want to have Yeshua live in your heart, like in the heart of Matan and Raphael?"

Adi and Yuval jumped up and said, "Yes, we do, we do!"

"Okay, let's pray together. Repeat after me, 'Father in heaven,'..."

"Father in heaven," they repeated, in Hebrew.

"'Forgive me for all my sins,...'"

"Forgive me for all my sins."

I'm asking you today to come into my heart,...'"

"I'm asking you to come into my heart," they repeated.

"'I'm asking you to come into my heart, to save me, and to live with me forever.'..."

Oh, my children accepted the Lord. Their little faces were radiant and they began to laugh, praising and worshipping God!

Now we were in the truck with Baruch, heading toward the water park. It would be a sight to behold — a new water park right in the desert! It was a prophecy coming true in

Israel, for the prophet Isaiah said there would be "streams of water in "the desert."

The only problem was that both Baruch and I had been out of jobs for months by now. We'd been able to survive just by faith, by the grace of God and by miracles. This water park was pretty expensive, but I was trusting that due to my being a tour guide, we'd be able to go in free, or pay very little.

I said to Adi honestly, "Adi, you know, I don't know how we're going to get in, because we don't have enough money to pay for the tickets. So please don't be disappointed if we don't manage to visit the water park. We'll do something else instead."

Adi said sternly, "Mommy, did you pray?"

"Sure, Adi. I prayed that God would make a way for us to get in."

Adi rebuked me. "Well, mommy, if you prayed, why are you doubting? If you prayed and believed God, we are going to get in!"

Ha! My daughter had more faith than I did! This little six-year-old knew more about God than I. She said the truth — that if I had prayed, there was nothing to worry about. Of course God would answer my prayers!

We spent the most beautiful day in the water park.

******

"You will never see the children again as long as I live!" Danny shouted at me. "I'm tired of Yuval coming home singing all these songs to Messiah. You cannot continue indoctrinating these children. You cannot teach them any more about the Messiah!"

"Danny, the only one who will forbid me to see my children is the Almighty. I don't care what you say. It is what the Lord says that matters." I was able to answer him calmly, yet very, very sternly. "In my home my children will learn about the Lord. In your home, you teach them what you want, but in mine they are going to learn to worship God, and that's the end of the matter."

He was furiously indignant. He would have liked to beat me again as he had other times before, but he knew there was something within me that gave me strength. What he didn't know was that I was surrounded by the mighty angels of God. I knew I had protection from God. This time the man could not touch me! He could not bruise me! He knew that he couldn't go any further.

Toward the end of the week I prayed, "Lord, I thank you for opening Danny's heart to allow me to see the children again. Thank you, Lord, that you are the only one who can allow me, or forbid me, and nothing can hinder my relationship with my children. I pray this in the name of Yeshua."

Then I dialed Danny's number and said, "Danny, I'm coming to pick up the children for the weekend."

As meekly as a pussy cat Danny said, "All right." God had changed his heart!

That happened time after time, week after week. God would change his heart every time I stood firm. I had decided that no matter what threats he made, I would not stop teaching my children about the Lord. The Bible says, "Train up your child in the way he should go, and when he is old he will not depart from it."

I knew I didn't have much time with them. Baruch and I were leaving for Bible school in America soon, in obedience to God. Then I would have to leave my children and not see them again for who knows how long. I would train them the way they should go, and they would not depart from it. They would not go into witchcraft or the occult. They would not have the sin of unbelief. They would know the Lord, and they would grow with Him.

"Yes!"

My days with Adi and Yuval were numbered, for we were rapidly approaching April.

We had already been married by the rabbis a few months before. However, we would not leave the country until after the public Messianic wedding.

Our wedding day was to be April the 8th, and it was now only a week away. The things Baruch and I had put for sale were almost completely sold. We didn't have a dime to pay for our flights. Neither did we have a dime to pay for the wedding celebration that the Holy Spirit had told us to have in the Promenade restaurant that overlooks the whole of Jerusalem. It was to be an open wedding for all to see. It would also be very expensive, for we would have to pay for the people to be treated with the best food available, a full five-course meal.

I was getting nervous about it. "Baruch, can you come pray with me?" I asked. "Either God gives us the money, or we don't go anywhere!" April was rapidly approaching and I had already told the children, "Mommy's going to leave soon." I did not want to play with their emotions, saying one thing, and doing another.

Earnestly I prayed, "Lord, you have to cause the money to come!" Of course God was not moved by me. He had his own timing concerning the money. He was making us learn to trust him, even though in the natural nothing was happening.

We met with the pastor the Sunday before the wedding and with the worship leader, planning the last details. We were having two pastors marry us, one a Gentile and one a Jew, representing the unity in the body of Messiah between Jew and Gentile.

After the rehearsal we loaded Baruch's green truck. It had been for sale too, but no one wanted to buy it. We took off, not knowing that the devil was waiting for us at the next corner!

A woman lost control of her car and drove straight into our truck! She smashed the front end of her car completely, totaling her car. Praise God, no one got hurt, but our truck was banged up.

That truck was the only possession we had left. Selling it was perhaps the only way we could afford to buy tickets to Hawaii and America. Now it was dented!

A woman came to me that day in the church at the Y.M.C.A. building. This is the church Baruch and I attended in Jerusalem. She said, "Dominiquae, the Lord has told me to do something special for you. I'm a beautician. On the day before you get married, I want to pamper you for 24 hours, give you all the massages, and all the beauty treatments that a queen would have before her wedding."

I hugged her. "Thank you! This is a blessing from God. I would love that!

Saturday came, the day before the wedding. We were excited about the wedding, but we had a lot of mixed emotions. We were to be leaving for Hawaii on April 9th, the day after the wedding. We had ordered the tickets by faith, though it was just two days away and we still couldn't pay for them! Nor did we have a dime to pay for our wedding.

The hardest thing had been done, I had told the children we were leaving. I'll never forget what Adi said to me: "Momma, I don't want you to leave." My heart was torn. O dear God would Adi ever understand why I left her? The pain in my heart was very deep as I tried to sound cheerful. "The first thing I'll do when I get to America will be to send you a Barbie doll house." That seemed to take her little six-year-old mind off the subject. Yet all of our hearts were bleeding that day.

I knew that if I obeyed God in His call on my life, He would some day put us together again. I wished I had my children in my custody. Then I could have taken them with me.

I knew that their father would never release them to me. "Over my dead body!" Danny's words seemed to ring in my ears. "But God knows," I said to myself, "He is working out a bigger plan than we can comprehend now."

We had packed everything we would take. We had given up the apartment. We were already staying in the home of some friends. We were already legally married, but had not yet had the celebration with Messianic Jews, and the blessing from the two pastors.

We had mixed emotions because we had never seen God working such a tremendous financial miracle. At least I hadn't. I had only been saved for a year and a half.

It was the day before the wedding. Baruch wanted to call some friends in the farther north of Israel who had once offered to buy his truck, but they hadn't been able to afford the $4,500 we were asking. They could only afford monthly payments, and that wasn't good enough for us. He felt he should call them again, but I didn't want him to.

He did it anyway. Greg, on the other end of the line asked, "Baruch, is your truck still for sale?"

Baruch said, "Yes." He knew that because of the insurance, the truck could be repaired and be in good condition again. God had told us to sell it for $4,500, and it's better to obey than to sacrifice.

Greg said, "We're going to buy your truck. We're coming to the wedding tomorrow, bringing the money to give to you then. We've been blessed by a German baroness," he explained. "She's given us $4,500 to buy a car or a truck, so we can take her around. She loves us, and wants us to serve her in that way, driving her all over the place. A truck is better than a car, because it's big enough for our whole family. Besides, this way we can bless you too. Receiving this money has been a miracle for us!"

Imagine Baruch's face! He was beaming! His face was radiating with more joy than I had seen for the last several weeks! I didn't know what he was talking about, but when he hung up the phone, and told me the story, I began jumping up and down, praising God and saying, "This is amazing! Amazing! The day before our wedding, two days before we leave!" That ugly green truck, that's gone through an accident just a week ago, has sold for $4,500 to people who couldn't afford it! Because of a German baroness who loved them and wanted them to drive her around!

God Almighty, who is all-powerful, is never late when he promises something. He's not too weak to move mountains for his people when they pray! We were shocked and amazed, and rejoicing!

Baruch and I had decided not to see each other again that day. He had not seen my wedding dress. It was designed by the inspiration of the Holy Spirit to look like a priestly gown. It was white, with a special sash, all made by hand.

Baruch left me that day with the beautician so she could make a beautiful woman out of me. We would not see each other again until the wedding day. I was full of fabulous amazement as I received the 24-hour treatment from her. I was treated like a queen, with massages and every type of cream you can imagine to make me into a beautiful bride for Baruch Bierman.

Chapter 30

Dancing Down The Aisle

"Again I will build you, and you shall be rebuilt o virgin of Israel! You shall again be adorned with your tambourines, and shall go forth in the dances of those who rejoice." Jeremiah 31:4

I was very nervous. I looked gorgeous. The beautician had taken care of me beautifully. I hadn't looked so good in years, probably never, because I'd never been married having the Holy Spirit of God living within me. I felt like a bride pure and holy, a virgin bride who would marry for the first time in her life. I knew God was with me. I knew that everyone could see what a tremendous work He'd done in my life.

The guests were all arriving at the Promenade restaurant. Many onlookers who were not guests were watching in expectancy. Israelis love weddings. Whenever they can gather to watch a wedding, they will come, especially if it is an outdoor wedding like ours.

I was standing at the back of the Promenade restaurant with my three bridesmaids. They were wearing dancing attire and carrying tambourines. They would be dancing around me. Rather than walking down the aisle, I would be dancing down the aisle! I would dance unto the Lord, to the music of

"The Spirit and the Bride say, 'Come!'", from the book of Revelation.

This was to be a prophetic wedding, because indeed, the Spirit and the Bride were saying, "Come!" to the people of Israel. "Come to your Messiah. Recognize Yeshua, the Messiah of Israel, as your Messiah."

Baruch and I would be representing the Bridegroom and the Bride, even the Lord and the Church getting married. There would be many people looking on, seeing that this wedding looked so Jewish to them, and yet seeing that it had things that were different. They would admire the wedding.

I had not realized that God was planning this to be a wedding of evangelism! Nor did I know that during the ceremony, some of our beloved friends would go to the onlookers and pass out Bibles. These people were being ministered to and having the Good News preached to them, while we were being blessed by the pastors as bride and bridegroom. God is so good. He didn't miss one little moment in making sure that our lives counted for him.

The music had begun. Baruch looked handsome. He was dressed in beautiful attire, like a talit, (a Jewish prayer shawl made into a robe), woven all by hand, such as would be used in the third temple. He looked different, and special.

And I looked like a queen, fit for the King of kings, a princess right out of heaven, and I felt like one too!

The music had started. Baruch Habah beshem Adonai, — "Blessed is he who comes in the name of the Lord." Before he left this world Yeshua had said, "Jerusalem, Jerusalem, people of Israel. You will not see me again until you say, 'Blessed is He who comes in the name of the Lord."

With this prophetic song, Baruch entered the wedding canopy to wait for his bride. The pastors were there. The people were there. Everything was ready for the wedding.

Then my music began: "The Spirit and the Bride say 'Come.'" When the music began, my bridesmaids prayed for me, laying hands on me so that I'd be peaceful.

I held my bouquet in my hands; my bridesmaids surrounded me, dancing around me as I began dancing down the aisle. I danced an interpretive dance unto the Lord, accompanied by this beautiful song of praise calling people to come into the kingdom of God.

After I completed the dance, I walked the last few steps to where the wedding canopy was, arriving right in front of Baruch.

"Dominiquae, do you take Baruch...." I said, "YES!"

"Baruch, do you take Dominiquae.." He said, "YES"

The words of eternal life, the words of an eternal marriage, were pronounced over us. Now for the first time in my life, I was married with the blessing of God.

I would be able to establish a home in Israel which would be indestructible, because the God of Israel would be in its center.

No longer was it Baruch Bierman and Dominiquae Albala. Now it was Baruch and Dominiquae Bierman as one flesh, one person, working together for God, forming one family.

I had never walked this road before, but I knew God had called me to marry this man, and God would make sure that this marriage would succeed.

Before the blessings were given a song of praise and worship was sung and played by the praise-and-worship team headed by Elishevah and Yuval. We lifted our hands to the Lord as the whole congregation, the invited guests and the onlookers, sang with us:

"Yes!"

More love, more power, more of you in our hearts,
We will worship you with all our might.
We will worship you with all of our soul,
For you are our Lord!

Epilogue

A few hours after their wedding ceremony, Baruch and Dominiquae found themselves on a plane taking them directly to Hawaii, just as the Lord had spoken.

The money needed came right in the middle of the wedding ceremony. Also, just before they left, they counted the money given as wedding gifts, and found that God had given them exactly the amount they had needed to pay for their wedding. Thus they left with no debts to the restaurant.

On that plane heading for America, they started a new life, a life of serving God together, a life of ministry together, a life that would take them down many different roads, through many miraculous situations, and adventures in God.

They would be used by the Messiah to bring reconciliation between Jews and Christians, and between the God of Israel and people everywhere through the perfect blood sacrifice of Yeshua the Messiah. They would proclaim to Israel the eternal words of God through the prophet Jeremiah:

> "Behold the days are coming, says the Lord, when I will make a new covenant with the house of Israel and with the house of Judah not according to the covenant that I made with their fathers in the day that I took them by the hand to bring them out of the land of Egypt, My covenant which they broke, though I

was a husband to them, says the Lord. But this is the covenant that I will make with the house of Israel after those days, says the Lord; I will put my law in their minds and write it on their hearts, and I will be their God and they shall be My people." Jeremiah 31:31-33

Through the power, of God Baruch and Dominiquae would be used to bring physical and emotional healing to many families and individuals throughout the world. She that had been torn by life and sin became an instrument in God's hands to bring healing and forgiveness.

Dominiquae is today an internationally known writer, preacher and travelling prophet. She and her husband, Baruch, lead a powerful apostolic ministry from Israel to the Nations with disciples in many different countries. The name of their ministry is:

Kad-Esh MAP, which means "Vessel of Fire" in Hebrew. MAP is for Messianic, Apostolic and Prophetic.

They want you to know that what God did for them through faith in Jesus, He can also do for you as you invite him into your lives.

A special message to you, the reader:

Yes!

"Yes" is one of the smallest words with the biggest meaning. One "yes" can change an entire life. If I wouldn't have said "yes" to Yeshua, (Jesus), I would probably be dead by now or emotionally crippled for life. Worse than that I would be on the road to eternal destruction.

The word "yes" can determine your destiny!

Please pray this "yes prayer":

"Yes Yeshua, (Jesus), I believe that you are the Son of God and that you rose from the dead. Come into my heart, forgive all of my sins and make me a child of the God of Israel forever. I renounce all the works of the devil, including all occult and witchcraft practices. Please heal me and deliver me from all evil. Fill me with your Holy Spirit and with your love and teach me how to walk with God. Amen."

If you prayed this prayer you are on the road to eternal life!

The Bible says that if you believe in your heart that Yeshua, Jesus Christ, is the Son of God, and that God raised him from the dead, and if you confess this with your mouth, then you will be saved.

The Bible says that He broke the curse that was upon your life by paying for all of your sins upon the cross. So in the authority bestowed upon me as His child and servant I pray:

"In the name of Yeshua, I break all the curses that have been upon your life and command all evil spirits, including evil familiar spirits, to leave your life and become part of the footstool of Yeshua. I forbid any demonic activity in your life. Amen."

Now with peace in your heart, find a congregation of people, Jews and Gentiles, who love the Lord Jesus and are free to worship under the anointing of his Holy Spirit. They will minister to you and disciple you in the ways of God.

I also encourage you right now to get a Bible and begin reading it. The best thing, if you want to know about the Lord Jesus, who is called in the Hebrew language Yeshua, is to read the gospels. The gospel of Matthew is especially helpful for Jewish people. It is helpful to read the book of

Acts, for then you will understand the power of God that can come into your life, and you can receive the baptism in the Holy Spirit.

If you are Jewish and want to receive the Messiah through the Tanach, which is commonly called the Old Testament, ask God to reveal himself to you as you read. Isaiah, chapter 53, depicts the Messiah and his death for our sins. Psalm 22 prophetically describes his crucifixion. Micah 5 tells where he was to be born. Isaiah 7:14 tells how he is to be born of a virgin.

I encourage you to seek the Messiah in the pages of the Bible, the Tanach and the New Testament, not in any external book. The Tanach is the book that God left us, as Jews, as a legacy. Talk to your God and say, "God, show me the Messiah in the pages of my Bible", and He will!

I encourage you to seek God with all of your heart. Make sure that you are on the right road to eternal life, which is also a road that leads to a brand new life in this present world. I encourage you to know my God, the one who has made me free. In the name of Jesus the Messiah, Yeshua HaMashiach, I bless you this day. Shalom!

Contact Details

For more information on other books and music produced by Dominiquae Bierman please go to www.dominiquaebierman.com

Daily TV program on GBN at 10 AM EST Monday-Friday

"REVIVAL CRY"

Go to www.gbn.cc or www.kad-esh.org for details

For Ministry information please contact:

karenmap@netvision.net.il

www.kad-esh.org

Kad-Esh Map Ministries USA
P.O. Box 7692
Salem, Oregon 97303
USA

USA telephone: 1-800-443-3246

USA Fax: 1-866-571-5414

Kad-Esh MAP Ministries Israel
P.O. Box 590
Jerusalem 91004
Israel

Israel telephone +972 523 781 553

Other Books and Music Produced

Music

Revival Cry CD

This moving new CD will cause you to pray in song from the depth of your heart, to praise with Hebrew beat and to receive a new fresh wind of revival into all your dry places. Expect deep healing and an encounter with "The God of Heaven and Earth". Sung in English and Hebrew.

Key of Abraham CD

This is a wonderful new CD with new songs given to Dominiquae Bierman by the Holy Spirit during her Apostolic Journeys. These wonderful songs will inspire you to love Israel and the Jewish Roots of the Faith. The music is in Hebrew, Spanish and English.

Uru (Awake) CD

This debut album consists of songs God gave her during "Prophetic Praise Watches" in Jerusalem. Uru is full of the anointing of God! Sung in Hebrew with easy sing-along English transliteration and translation, so that you don't have to speak Hebrew to join in!

Books

THE HEALING POWER OF THE ROOTS
Why is it so important to preach the Jewish Roots of the faith to the church? I asked the Father and He said - "it is a matter of life and death". This book is a MUST for every believer.

SHEEP NATIONS
Imparting the deepest vision in the Heart of the Father for the salvation of the nations and based on a visitation of the Lord to Bishop Dominiquae Bierman in Chile.

GRAFTED IN
A revolutionary book calling the Church to an uncompromised walk of holiness! This is a mentoring manual that everyone should have next to their Bibles!

STORMY WEATHER
Is there any connection between Gaza Disengagement and Katrina and the Storms? Repentance from "The Israel Issue" can STOP Global warming from destroying your city! The facts related here are EYE OPENING! Do not miss it! A serious message is written in the winds of "Stormy Weather". With a possibility for a flooding revival

THE MAP REVOLUTION
Why is it that revival does not come? What can you do to break through the barrier into End Time Revival? This is the book that will change your perspective and put you on the right track.

YESHUA IS THE NAME
The awesome Prophetic Restoration of the original Hebrew name of Messiah. It will change your life and the life of millions!

THE BIBLE CURE FOR AFRICA
The challenging relationship between Africa and Israel is the KEY for the restoration of ALL of Africa and those of African descent. This book should be in the hands of RULERS!

TOURS

ISRAEL TOURS SPONSORED BY THE AUTHOR
Life changing, comprehensive, anointed, exciting...Truly nothing like it!

See, feel, understand and fall in love with the Miracle called Israel!

Dominiquae Bierman has over 25 years of experience organizing and guiding small and large groups through God's Holy Land.

You cannot afford to miss this unique experience. Go to www.purim4000.org

Printed in the United States
131395LV00002B/484-678/P